PERQUÍN MUSINGS

a gringo's journey in el salvador

Ron Brenneman

PERQUÍN MUSINGS

a gringo's journey in el salvador

First Edition

Published 2013

Library of Congress Control Number:

ISBN 978-0-9885921-0-0

Dedicated to those who have brought me full circle, to my wife Ena Catalina and our children, Jeovana, Michael, Andrew and Sarah Rohana

A special thank you to family and friends who have supported me throughout the years and held me in your thoughts and prayers

I hope this explains a bit of what, how and why.

Two individuals I want to recognize for their contributions towards this book are Kristy Nolan and Don Warnick for editing and proofing.

PERQUÍN MUSINGS

a gringo's journey in el salvador

Ron Brenneman

PERQUÍN MUSINGS

Contents **page**

Contents **page**

Prologue

The shooting picked up again and this time included grenades, either launched by the soldiers on my left or dropped out of the helicopter screaming by. No way to tell for sure. The guerrillas on my right responded immediately with the slow heavy tat-tat of the AK-47s and I was caught in the middle.

"End of the line," I thought as I dove behind of a stack of firewood and sucked in a mouthful of the dry white volcanic dust. Shrapnel and bullets were cutting through the tin siding of the house I was lying next to.

"Better off out here than inside," I thought.

As the pace of fire picked up even more, I begin to wonder, "Did I go a little too far out on a limb this time and how in the world did a Delaware farm boy get himself into this spot anyway?"

It was 1989 in San Salvador, on the seventh day of the guerrilla offensive. I was a humanitarian aid worker with the Lutheran World Federation, and I was way out of my element.

I have been very fortunate. Life has been very generous in providing opportunities to step out of my element and in over my head, to sink or swim.

Along with that, of course, is the required self-examination of pre-existing concepts, truths and beliefs. Some have helped me to swim, others needed to be discarded in order to not sink. Stripped of their traditional trappings, beliefs become clear, with new meaning. They are no longer the mechanical *faith of our fathers*.

The Salvadoran Civil War lasted from 1981 through to the signing of the Peace Accords on the 16th of January, 1992. Categorized as a *low intensity conflict* with-in the framework of the East-West Cold War, a US backed Salvadoran government, in transition from military dictatorship to an incipient democracy, faced a loosely organized group of socialist revolutionaries in a war which would take over 75,000 lives.

The dramatic human tragedy caused by the human rights abuses and mass assassinations of the civilian population sprang very quickly into international headlines. Dozens of humanitarian and church organizations heeded the call for help and arrived to give emergency assistance, provide human rights monitoring and physical presence. Hundreds of volunteers from all over the world made the courageous decision to stand by and share with the Salvadoran people in this time of need.

While assigned specific tasks in emergency assistance to affected communities, many volunteers soon found themselves immersed in a world gone mad, and without the possibility of remaining detached. Personal values and emotional strength were sorely tested in this highly charged situation.

All who went through this conflictive period of Salvadoran history were marked deeply by their experience.

Perquín Musings is the recollection and thoughts of one of those volunteers.

I AM

Time spirals by
Truths, so carefully constructed and defended
Time Locked
Anchored to the distant past
Lessons only
No longer apply

Belief, stripped of the Beautifully Embellished Facts,
becomes a Lie

Only time enduring Truth:
I AM!

Ego-centered? Of course! That is what this civilization is about. Our big question is what to do with ego. It seems we are divided into only two camps: Those, who like sheep, stick with the flock, denying ego and those who run with the wolves.

No ground yet staked out for the mature ego. Most just standing by, watching greed break down all socio-economic structures, contrived and tried, and as sheep, hunker down hoping not to be noticed.

The path is what we leave behind.
Before us all possibility, all potential!
If we are following a marked path, it belongs to someone else; it is not ours.

The Straight and Narrow,
a winding treacherous path.
Mysticism tempting us into the clouds, Materialism pulling us back down.
Conservatism to the Right, Liberalism to the Left
Middle-ground is a lukewarm trap!
Each a path that circles back on itself going nowhere.

I AM NOT a compromise, not middle ground. I AM the right action at the precise moment, regardless of the relativity of the powers that be. The Straight and Narrow is just that: straight and narrow. The illusion of winding occurs as temporal definitions snake back and forth, from left to right and back again. We need times of enlightenment and we need to get our feet on the ground too. Sometimes the right is right, sometimes the left is right. Often, they are both missing the point. We give up and fail when we allow ourselves to be defined and fixed in social, political or even religious terms.

Where I'm From

Where I'm from is no longer a geographical location. The oft asked question, "How often do you get back home?" normally gets shrugged off with a curt, "Well, I'm at home here" or "Not too often."

Back home is ping-pong out in the shop, tinkering with motorcycles, scrapple and eggs in the morning, shooting off shotguns on New Year's Eve, Aunt Olive's blueberry muffins, Lydia's strawberry pie, Wilson's Friday-night Auction, small mouth bass at Blair's Pond, pot lucks and family dinners. Everything has changed, cornfields paved over for malls, interstate roads for beach traffic and outlet stores. Food comes from the grocery, gardens are ornamental and the current family feud has broken up the pot lucks. It would take time travel to *get back home.*

"If it's worth doing, it's worth doing right," was my father's most repeated phrase, at least the one I remember clearest from growing up. The other, whenever we left home was, "Remember now where you're from."

The first phrase, while not always obtainable, has developed into a constant measuring stick as I move on in this journey. The second frankly comes in cycles: first a rejection of status quo, then an excursion out into the real world and finally coming back and incorporating those experiences into *where I'm from.*

A carpenter/builder by trade, I grew up in southern Delaware, on the east coast, as part of a small Mennonite community. It was a sheltered, safe upbringing. The church was mostly extended family, with little difference between family reunions and church pot lucks. My brothers and I attended public school, which was our window into the world. However the concept of *being in the world but not of the world* was ingrained in us, creating an invisible yet unmoving boundary regarding how much we could become involved.

Service to others is a fundamental cornerstone of the Mennonite Church, so I naturally joined in volunteer activities as was asked of us during those formative years. Before settling down to adult responsibilities, young people within the church were encouraged to go into missions or voluntary service. So after graduating high school, I joined with the Mennonite Voluntary Service as a volunteer worker. From mid-1977 through 1979, I worked in Champaign-Urbana, Illinois, as a carpenter involved in the rehabilitation of low-income housing. In 1980, I volunteered for short-term service in a temporary shelter care center in Ocean City, Maryland, prior to enrolling in Eastern Mennonite College.

While I enjoyed some aspects of college, I left before completing the first year, having decided that my future education was not necessarily contained in a classroom.

A common trait of mine, perhaps my most consistent one, is to first step in over my head and then begin to learn the ropes.

In 1983, while pondering whether to expand my one-man carpentry operation into a small business, I decided to put the decision off temporarily and take one more term of voluntary service, since I had not yet been *overseas*. I called Mennonite Central Committee (MCC), asked where the next post was for a carpenter overseas, requested it and then looked for an atlas to locate Honduras.

Terms and Players: *As defined within the context of this book, only. Perquín Musings contains the perceptions and understanding of the author and speaks to the effects of conflict on human nature. It is not to be taken as a history refercnce work.*

AKA: or AK-47 is the Kalashnikov assault rifle.

CRS: Catholic Relief Services. CRS is the relief and aid development agency of the United States Catholic Conference.

Death Squads: Para-military forces operating with impunity assassinated an estimated 30,000 Salvadorans suspected to be subversives or guerrilla sympathizers, prior to and during the civil conflict.

El Mozote: On the 10th of December, 1981, the US trained Actlacatl battalion massacred between eight hundred and a thousand civilians in and around the hamlet of El Mozote, in the north-east province of Morazán. This book explores the idiosyncrasy of an eyewitness and in no manner questions the veracity of the event. For a full historical account, please see Mark Danner's "The Massacre at El Mozote."

ERP: The People's Revolutionary Army was formed in 1972 by a group of middle-class university students and young radical Christians. They developed a radical national liberation and anti-imperialist stance. It was radical to the point that they included the Soviet Union as an imperialist power. This of course would be a point of contention in their relationship with the PCS and FPL, who considered them to be a loose cannon and sorely lacking in Marxist-Leninist theory. The strategy of the ERP was that of popular insurrection sparked by focused guerrilla warfare, which would be closer to the strategy implemented by Castro in the Cuban revolution. They were considered the most military capable member of the FMLN.

Their base of operation was the north of the Morazán province, as well as on the El Tigre volcano of Usulután.

FARN: The Armed Forces of National Resistance, better known as the RN, formed in 1975 and was an offshoot of the ERP. An internal purge resulting from clashing ideologies was intensified by the paranoia of Alejandro Mira, the first leader of the ERP. The infighting led to the death of the now-famous Salvadoran poet, Rogue Dalton, and several other original members of the ERP, as well as the desertion of Alejandro. The resulting split fell somewhat along the political versus military stances within the leadership. In general terms, the political sector went with the RN and the militaristic elements stayed with the ERP. This action of course heightened and reinforced the reputation being gained by the ERP.

The RN basically maintained the same strategy after the split and actually worked closely with the ERP in military operations and generally closed ranks with the ERP in political discussions within the FMLN. Idcologically moderate, they tended towards a social-democratic stance. There bases of operation were in the north of La Union, part of Morazán and pockets in Usulután.

FMLN: The Farabundo Marti National Liberation Front was an umbrella organization formed by five independent revolutionary groups. While all of the groups grew out of the same root, namely the organizing work of the Salvadoran Communist Party in the late 60s and early 70s, they varied widely in ideological terms and in insurrectional strategy. The actual forming of one organization from such diverse groups, in October of 1980, came about at the insistence of Fidel Castro who grew tired of receiving individual requests for aid from each one. Withholding arms shipments until a unified front was founded was all the coercion necessary.

FPL: The Popular Forces of Liberation was formed in 1970 by a group from the PCS who had grown impatient with the party's resistance to armed insurrection. This group, made up of clergy and leaders of the Teacher's Union and Trade and Farm Worker's organizations, were attracted by the Vietnamese strategy of *prolonged people's struggle.* The FPL emphasized community and social organization, although they did field a large contingent of combat-ready fighters. Their base of operation became the mountains in the province of Chalatenango, in north-central El Salvador.

Lutheran World Federation: LWF is an organization of Lutheran Churches with members in 79 countries throughout the world, headquartered in Geneva.

MCC: Mennonite Central Committee. MCC is the relief and aid development agency of the North American Mennonite and Brethren churches. They focus on peace and conflict resolution.

NGOs: Non-Governmental Organizations. Commonly humanitarian service groups, church organizations and human rights monitoring.

UNHCR: United Nations High Commissioner for Refugees. The UNHCR provided protection through the extension of refugee status to the Salvadorans fleeing the war and administrated the refugee camps in Honduras. They managed the diplomatic negotiations directly with the Honduran government and contracted local and international NGOs for the required services, goods and assistance to the refugee population.

PCS: The Salvadoran Communist Party dates its history to the 1930s, to Farabundo Marti, the leader of the failed indigenous uprising which resulted in the killing of over thirty thousand Salvadoran peasants. The PCS was a legal political party in El Salvador up through the 70s and was resistant to joining the armed struggle. It was not until Moscow issued the directive to get on the train before it left the station that the PCS reluctantly joined the revolution and formed the Armed Forces of Liberation (FAL).

The PCS was Moscow-line communist and the FAL was a rigid formal military structure, the only group with defined officer and enlisted ranks. The base of operation of the FAL was the area of Guazapa, a volcanic range just north of the capital. They also probably had the largest urban guerrilla contingent of any of the organizations, within San Salvador.

PRTC: The Revolutionary Party of Central American Workers was formed in 1977 by a group of intellectuals with Trotsky leanings. The by-far smallest armed guerrilla organization of the FMLN, the PRTC held little territory of its own, often camping out in areas under control of the larger organizations. The need to overcome the perception of small and weak did lead the PRTC to carry out daring actions, some of which were unsanctioned and caused political backlash, such as the infamous *Massacre in the Zona Rosa*, on June 19, 1985, in which four US Marines, two US businessmen and six other civilians were gunned down at a sidewalk café in an exclusive San Salvador neighborhood.

Radio Venceremos: A clandestine rebel radio broadcast from the war zone which provided news, music and guerrilla propaganda to the outside world.

Segundo Montes: Named in honor of one of the Jesuit priests slain by the Salvadoran military on November 16, 1989, Segundo Montes is the community of former refugees repatriated from the Colomoncagua camp in Honduras.

Honduras

Colomoncagua

In July of 1983, I arrived in Honduras as a volunteer with Mennonite Central Committee (MCC). My work was in Salvadoran Refugee Camps on the Honduras border, under the coordination of the UNHCR. MCC was in charge of the infrastructure projects, including housing, workshops, water systems and roads in the refugee camps of Mesa Grande, Colomoncagua and San Antonio. I was assigned to housing in Colomoncagua and San Antonio, the destination and temporary home of some 12,000 people fleeing the war in the north-east Salvadoran provinces of Morazán, San Miguel and Cabañas.

Women, children and elderly people began fleeing the combat zones in El Salvador for the relative safety of neighboring Honduras as early as 1980. The growing numbers, as well as reports of abuse and abductions by Salvadoran para-military forces and the Honduran military, led to the arrival of the UNHCR in 1982. This led to the establishment of three major refugee camps in Honduras: Mesa Grande, with a population of 12,000 refugees, Colomoncagua with 8,400 refugees and San Antonio with 1,200 refugees. By 1988, these camps had grown by an estimated thirty percent, as more refugees trickled in.

A little noted camp was Buenos Aires. Located on the soccer field in the town of Colomoncagua, it contained a small group of Salvadorans varying in numbers from forty to one hundred. These refugees were considered to be government sympathizers and were allowed freedom of movement in Honduras. With no military control at all over the camp, these Salvadorans were free to leave at will, to travel, work and do business.

The three main camps were considered to hold guerrilla sympathizers and families of guerrillas. They were basically concentration camps under Honduran military control.

The first impression of coming into the Colomoncagua camp will always stay with me. The sky was crystal blue with puffy white clouds racing by in the crisp mountain breeze. The winding gravel road ran through pines singing with the wind. Then, it dropped down into the valley to meet a rising sweetly pungent aroma of overcrowded camp life, wood-fires, sweat and outhouses. An ever increasing low hum turned into the laughter and shouting of hundreds and hundreds of children playing.

My job was to oversee the transition from tents and temporary shelters to semi-permanent housing. The Honduran government, while agreeing to allow refugee camps along the border, was fearful of long-term settlements being established.

They constantly brought up the example of the permanent refugee camps in Palestine, and would not authorize the building of permanent structures. I designed a simple structure of pine posts painted with burnt oil, ship lapped green pine siding and galvanized roofing, a model that is still known today as *Ron's house* in Morazán.

While working with the Salvadoran construction teams, six in Colomoncagua and one in San Antonio, I began to know each individual, meet their families and to hear accounts of what they had been through.

The resilience of human nature in the face of adversity defies comprehension. Everyone I met had lost a family member to the war. I met a lot of older folks who had lost four, five, up to seven sons or daughters. Everyone had someone they were anxiously waiting to hear from or to hear that they were still alive.

As I began to know the people, I couldn't help but be reminded of folks back home, the same personalities, gestures, generosity, aspirations and hopes. The circumstances in which the refugees found themselves was the only difference from the folks back home and I pondered on whether *we* would have such strength if faced with similar circumstances.

The camps grew as small groups of twenty to thirty persons would manage to slip through the Honduran military control at night. They were gaunt, grey-faced and frightened, even the children quieted down when they came out in the morning. They received food and medical attention immediately and after they were documented by the UNHCR, received an identity card that they carried at all times.

Under pressure from the Salvadoran government, in 1984, the Honduran government began a program to move the refugee camps from the Salvadoran border to the Honduran Atlantic coast. As the UNHCR began preparations for the move, the refugees started a movement opposing the plan which became internationally known.

Aid agencies and workers were naturally caught up in the debate and it practically divided the whole operation into two groups, those in favor of the move and those against it.

Within this context another debate arose among the Mennonite volunteers concerning our purpose in Honduras. MCC was in Honduras at the request of the Honduran Mennonite Church, which had already gone out on a limb to work with leftist refugees. We needed to take care to not endanger the local Mennonites further by taking a personal stance contrary to the church.

The debate centered on which was more important, the long-term relationship and support of the local Mennonite Church or the short-term support for Salvadoran refugees in temporary camps.

I favored supporting the refugees, so when the Honduran Mennonite Church signed a contract with the UNHCR and the government for the construction of new camps on the coast, MCC and I came to a mutually acceptable early termination agreement.

The surprise detention and subsequent deportation of one of the CRS workers opened a position with them in the same camps of Colomoncagua and San Antonio. So I stayed on to work with CRS.

The cultural diversity of aid workers in the refugee camps provided a window to the world, not only for the refugees themselves, but for those of us who had never left home before. The mixture of North American, French, Japanese, German, Spaniard, Bolivian, Irish, British and Nordics descending on a small mountain town of some three hundred inhabitants, made for interesting encounters, both in and out of the camp setting.

One morning arriving at the camp, we noticed everyone out along the road, whispering in small groups. Thinking that a security problem had occurred, we stopped to ask what had happened.

"We're not sure," was the reply. "But just a few minutes ago a naked white man came running through here... but no one was chasing him."

Turned out to be a North American aid worker out for a jog, wearing just shorts and running shoes. It took some explaining, but was gradually accepted as *normal* by the refugees.

CRS was the agency in charge of the workshop program within the camps. This entailed setting up training workshops with the dual purpose of training young people in a skill for their post-war lives, as well as for labor force in the production workshops, which provided most of the material needs for the camps. Workshop production included clothing, shoes and leather work, sleeping mats, hats, pottery, blacksmithing, tinsmithing, steel-work, mechanics, weaving, carpentry and rope and hammock making. The production from these workshops covered nearly ninety percent of the needs in the camps. I was tasked with supplying raw materials and teachers for the workshop program, as well as purchasing items we were unable to produce.

Life as a volunteer in the refugee camp was idyllic in many ways. Never had right and wrong been so marked out with clear lines and I was on the side of the oppressed. There was exotic international flavor, with shocking new ideas, new books, new music and comradeship.

Passion, pure and unrestrained by norms, on all levels: righteous outrage at injustice, vibrant identification with the downtrodden, companionship in tragedy and companionship in love. We were stripped to the essentials, with no television, no electricity, the nearest phone two hours away, and the nearest supermarket six hours away. It was life at its purest and finest.

The only common language used among the aid workers was Spanish, which was everyone's second tongue, including the Spaniards, given the huge difference in dialects between the provinces of Spain and Salvadoran Spanish. Smaller groups would converse in French or English, but group communication was all Spanish, which made for interesting and frustrating coordination.

For me personally, there were many firsts. My first plane ride was to Honduras. The first real city I lived in was in Tegucigalpa, where I went for language training and where I rode my first city bus. It was my first contact with Europeans and Central Americans.

My first Catholic girlfriend, M from Canada, introduced me to another series of firsts. Among them, my first wine out of a corked bottle, French bread, Brie cheese and espresso coffee.

It was a long way from living in a trailer on my brother's dairy farm in Powhatan, Virginia, where my idea of a good afternoon was to pick up two chili dogs and a six-pack on my way to fish in the river.

August Massacre

In August 1985, the Colomoncagua refugee camp came under military attack by the Honduran forces, reportedly with Salvadoran military participation. One young man and a two-month old girl were killed. An elderly man would die a few days later of wounds received. Dozens of refugees, mostly women and children, were wounded and ten men were taken prisoner.

While speeding to the end of the camp where the heavy shooting was going on, I ran into the line of ten men being taken out of the camp. I got out of the pickup and followed along. These men were sure they were being taken out for execution and some asked me to take their belongings to give to their families. The soldiers would not slow down and would not talk to me, and if one of the men slowed down to give me something, a soldier would hit him in the spine with a rifle butt.

After a walk of about twenty minutes, we came to a clearing where a helicopter was waiting. J, from the UNHCR, was already there trying to prevent the removal of the men. J, who was a playboy type, was fairly new to the job. He would show up at the camp wearing shorts, sandals, a headband and sunglasses. He really looked like he had gotten lost on the way to the beach. This day, however, he stood firm and kept repeating that he represented the UN and that the men could not be taken.

He took a position on one side of the helicopter; I took a position on the other side. Unfortunately we also got into a pushing match with the soldiers, were gassed and forcibly removed. The ten men began a long painful journey to the Honduran military garrison in Marcala. They were later deported to Canada, where some remain to this day. The next day J was sent to a new assignment in Africa, I was called in, had my hands slapped and promised to behave in the future.

It seems that sending unprepared and unaware young people into a highly volatile situation is nothing new. Armies do it, so why not humanitarian and church organizations? Would it really be that difficult to give some forewarning?

A couple of weeks after the attack, tensions were still running high. The majority of the aid workers had moved up to the camp in an effort to offer more protection. The Honduran army increased patrols within the camp limits, disrupting all semblance of normalcy. Our tasks were reduced to keeping the soldiers in sight as they patrolled and trying to keep the children from throwing rocks at them.

It was within this atmosphere that one of the Honduran Mennonite workers happened to find a pistol lying on the road within the refugee camp limits. I was walking from one sub-camp to another that morning, when D picked me up. He was the youngest of the local Mennonite workers and someone who seemed out of place, although I couldn't put my finger on the reason.

Midway between the camps, he stopped and pulled a pistol out of the glove compartment. Thrusting it at me, he said, "I found this on the road this morning. It must belong to the guerrillas. What should I do?"

I had my hands full of papers and didn't take the pistol. I had the distinct feeling he was looking for a reaction of some kind, perhaps expecting me to try to convince him to forget about it and to let me take it off his hands.

"Quien sabe, who knows," I shrugged. "It could be anyone's."

He turned the pistol in to the UNHCR.

That afternoon, I caught a ride to the camps with S, the Japanese UNHCR representative. He began to lament the situation, saying that the pistol was proof that the guerrillas were coming into the camp and that the refugees themselves were to blame for the military actions taken against them. He was taking the pistol to the authorities because he had no other recourse.

We were soon arguing heavily over his intended action and when I got out of the Jeep, I said "Just be careful what you do with that," and slammed the Jeep door.

The next day I was called in and reprimanded for threatening a UN officer. I clarified my remarks of course, and suggested that a language barrier may have caused the misunderstanding.

A local farmer called on the military garrison a few days later to report that he had lost his pistol while out drinking on horseback several nights before, so the potentially explosive situation was de-fused.

Volunteer Phases

Most volunteers go through three phases, if they stay around long enough.

First phase: Romantic identification with the group of people they are working with. Often starting with a righteous indignation at the treatment the group has been subject to. Depending on the circumstances, this phase will last from two to three years, often the entire period of the volunteer post.

Second phase: Cynicism and disillusionment from un-met expectations. Discovery of self-interest and unethical behavior among those formerly looked at with admiration. Many leave during this stage and become resentful that they have given up part of their life and energy to a people unworthy of that gift.

Third phase: Discovery that people everywhere are basically the same and that all systems depend on the people within them. No system is inherently good or evil, nor does it automatically convert those people within it to good or evil. This discovery allows one to step back from idealism and participate in local society. It also eliminates the concept of *back home* and *over there.*

The Church of San Fernando

On the road between the sub-camps of Los Quebrachos and Callejones, there was an outcrop looking over Morazán. It was out of camp limits, but I would often stop there and climb up to sit and watch and wonder about life on the other side. It was only three miles from the border, so large weapon fire was audible when close by and the aerial bombing from much further away. The only visible structure as a point of reference was the front of the Catholic Church in San Fernando, about ten miles away. Its large white face would brighten in the afternoon sun.

In January of 1984, the Kissinger Commission, under a mandate from the Reagan administration, recommended that Congress pass an immediate increase in military aid to El Salvador. This recommendation also basically abolished restraints established by Congress during Reagan's first term. These restraints included certification of improvement in human rights, less corruption and more efficiency. The military aid budget for 1984 increased to $197 million, up from the previous $82 million.

We received the news in Colomoncagua, before the ink was dry on the congressional agreement. Six Dragonfly jets screamed over the camp at treetop level, followed by twelve Huey helicopters jam packed with troops. As they disappeared over the ridge into Morazán, I ran to my Jeep and headed for the lookout.

This was the first use of a new tactic by the Salvadoran military. They were now crossing into Honduran airspace to make surprise sweeps back across the border into guerrilla-held territory.

The attack began before I reached the outcropping, the San Fernando area was billowing with black smoke by the time I could get a clear view. As I watched, the front of the church exploded into a dusty puff and disappeared.

The increase in military aid to El Salvador did have an effect, although not the desired one. Faced with a better equipped enemy with decent air power, the guerrillas broke their large contingents down into three to five person units and spread throughout the country. The aerial bombardment greatly increased but with questionable results. This was obvious even from our observation from the camps. Previously, a spotter plane would come out first, followed by one or two jets that would dive on specific targets and drop two 500-pound bombs. With the military aid increase, four planes would come out at once and almost randomly dump their bombs, to the point that it seemed they were doing periodic inventory reductions.

The Night Owl

In late 1984, the town of Colomoncagua received a mysterious visitor. He appeared one night and disappeared back into the night about six months later. In such a small town, it is impossible not to know what is going on.

At the time all aid workers lived in town. One doctor and two volunteers on a medical team were the only foreign presence authorized to be in the camps at night. The town itself was under military curfew, so no one could be out after dark. The curfew was enforced by a patrol of a dozen or so soldiers marching through the four streets of the town. We could not stand being penned up at night, of course, so when the patrol was on one street, the other three streets were full of shadows. You would see them flitting from house to house as aid workers had meetings, parties or just went out.

One morning everyone noticed a new wire antenna stretched from the military headquarters to the church tower. That night we got our first glimpse of the night owl. After curfew, stretching from sitting at his radio set all day, out came a sandy-haired, blue-eyed, North American-looking soldier wearing distinctive round glasses. He immediately became known as the *night owl.* He only came out at night and would never speak to us.

You could catch him unaware though by stepping out of the shadows quickly and asking "How you doing?"

A very polite "Very well, thank you" always slipped out before he could stop it.

Throughout the war in El Salvador, numerous attempts were made to locate and capture or destroy Radio Venceremos, a very effective propaganda tool for the guerrillas. It would seem that our friend, the night owl, was part of a larger operation to triangulate the radio signal.

The Ghost Plane

Not a lot to do at night in a small mountain town, with a curfew at sunset and no electricity. Not a lot of privacy either, with the number of international workers and the limited housing available.

The patio out back was a favorite place to chat and get away from the crowd. Clay tiles for drying coffee retain the heat from the sun and make for a comfortable place to lay back and watch the stars.

The night sky in Colomoncagua was incredible, no light pollution and the stars so big and close you could almost reach out and touch them.

Late one night, a girlfriend M and I went out back with a bottle of wine, some Brie cheese and a blanket to take the chill off. We were lying there watching the stars, when a plane the size of a DC3 slowly flew overhead, just above tree top level. Completely silent, so close we could feel the breeze from its passing but could not hear the engines. The doors were open, with a faint green/bluish light inside.

No way to be sure what it was doing, tracking the radio, looking for troop concentrations or mapping out the territory.

But for us, it was another of those constant reminders of the ongoing war in El Salvador, interrupting even a brief interlude of escape and enjoyment of something so simple and magnificent as the night sky over Colomoncagua.

El Salvador:
The War years

San Jorge

In late August of 1986, I arrived in El Salvador under contract with the Lutheran World Federation. I was to set up an agricultural project, coordinated with the Lutheran Church, in the small mountain town of San Jorge, on the slope of the Chaparrastique volcano in San Miguel.

The local Lutheran pastor, a wizened old guy, was a cross between witch doctor, clan leader and Man of God. He had his flock firmly under control. Church members would come to his home daily to leave a portion of their harvest, something from the market or a few hens. He always had a few rattlesnake carcasses drying on the roof to grind into powder for making his potions.

During the short time that I was in San Jorge, the pastor divided his time equally between running through the hills attending his flock or making deals and lying on his deathbed.

We were a group of five international workers, a Spanish teacher, a French teacher, a Spanish doctor, a French nurse and myself. Our work was spread throughout the community. As a group, the majority of the time we were together was spent sitting around the pastor's deathbed waiting for him to go one way or the other. In his lucid moments, he would call for more rattlesnake potion, spew up a black vomit and slip back under. On three separate occasions we thought he had died, but each time he would rise up and in no time be back at his routine.

San Jorge was hot; the only change in weather was between hot and dry, or hot and humid. It was one of those towns where the only sensible place to be at midday was in the hammock under a shade tree.

Unlike the Salvadorans I knew from the camps, the people of the town were not particularly friendly. This was a military garrison town. The garrison had not been attacked for some time and although the war activity could be heard only sporadically and from a distance, the townspeople still eyed us *internacionalistas* with suspicion.

As the first month went by, I settled into a routine of putting up with the heat and trying to get a program started. I had a vegetable plot going, some erosion control set up and a few rain water catchments in process. It was satisfactory but not particularly gratifying.

I did have some misgivings about working for a family business cloaked as a church. The housing also was a bit uncomfortable because the other volunteers had been there for some time, and I was the outsider breaking up their routine. I was coming from the cool climate of Colomoncagua, and dealing with the heat was rough, so the French nurse prancing around in a sheer baby doll nightie did not have the calming effect it was perhaps intended to have.

As I was mulling over the situation in my mind, something happened which would override any decision I might have made regarding my tenure and the French nurse. A major quake hit San Salvador.

Earthquake

On October 10 of 1986, an earthquake measuring 7.5 on the Richter scale, hit the city of San Salvador killing an estimated 1,500 people. In San Jorge, we had some side to side movement, but did not get the full impact of the situation until the news came over the radio. The next morning we headed for the capital to help where we could.

The drive into San Salvador was extremely chaotic. Utility lines were down, crevasses had to be bypassed and buildings were crumbled onto main roads with bodies emerging from the rubble.

The strong aftershocks had everyone in panic. For a full week, we all slept out on the street, abandoning the death traps that homes threatened to become, forming one big urban campground. There was an admirable show of generosity among neighbors with the sharing of food, clothing and water.

A unilateral truce was called by the FMLN to allow attention to be focused on the earthquake relief effort and a few guerrilla commanders took advantage of the chaotic situation to slip into the city and visit family that they hadn't seen in years.

I stayed in San Salvador to head up earthquake relief efforts for the Lutheran Church. Ironically, most of the hardest hit communities were temporary settlements set up for the homeless victims of the May 1965 earthquake. Indeed, most of the buildings that went down were structurally weakened in the earlier quake and only superficially patched up. The most dramatic case being the five-story Ruben Dario office building, which came down like a house of cards killing over three hundred. A further irony is that the Ruben Dario had been repaired by the construction firm of Jose Napoleon Duarte, President of El Salvador during the 1986 earthquake.

As we began the effort to provide emergency housing materials to the poor marginalized communities, we were asked for pine planks.

"Why do you want planking?" I asked, "We've got tin for roofing and siding and two-by-fours for the structure."

"We'll get to that," was the reply, "but first we need to bury the dead."

It took the first three days of the emergency effort just to supply the materials for coffins.

A friendly face

I was chosen by the Council of Churches in San Salvador to go to Guatemala and Honduras to buy materials for emergency housing for the earthquake victims. It was a fairly simple task. I was to buy as much tin roofing as I could get my hands on in Guatemala and then go to the state run mill in Honduras for lumber.

Late one afternoon I was summoned to the office of one of the organizations.

I was causally handed a plane ticket, two checks and told "Good luck."

The checks were from a Panama bank, each made out to a different woman I had never heard of and each for one hundred thousand dollars. The gentleman who presented me with the checks was already leaving the room when I asked where I was to find the women to endorse the checks.

"Oh, that's right," he said as he took the checks back. He glanced at the names and endorsed them himself.

I caught the last flight of the day to Guatemala, arriving around ten thirty at night. Coming out of the airport, I got strange vibes from the group of taxi drivers, so I jumped on a bus.

Guatemala City is fairly easy to get around. The streets are laid out nice and straight, so it is hard to get lost. I knew it well from previous trips. When the bus turned in the wrong direction, I got out and got my bearings.

It was one of those misty nights. The rain had just ended and steam was rising from the still warm pavement. There were no cars to be seen and not a taxi in sight. Everything was closed and I had fourteen blocks to walk in downtown Guatemala City.

I knew the worst thing I could do was stand around looking lost, so I strode down the middle of the street like I knew where I was going.

"How stupid can you get," I muttered to myself. Here I was, walking through the wrong side of town with two hundred thousand dollars in a silly little briefcase someone had loaned me for the trip.

An occasional car sped by on the next block. I heard police sirens in the distance, dogs fighting over scraps at the garbage bin and my footsteps echoing off the dark buildings. My shadow jumped from one side of the street to the other depending on which streetlights were burned out.

About four blocks from the hotel, the National Guard building blocks the street, so I turned left to bypass it. This National Guard was not your friendly neighborhood cop.

As I came up to the corner, a shadow stepped out of a doorway. My heart stopped.

It was just a poor old prostitute offering her services, but she was the friendliest face I had seen all night. I declined and thanked her for the offer. That brief encounter took the tension out of the night and I was still laughing at myself when I finally reached the hotel.

Truth stands by Itself

The massacre of over one thousand civilians on a December day in the hamlet of El Mozote is a cold hard fact. The political persuasion of the victims, as well as the political leaning of the observer, does not alter that fact in any manner. Neither is it altered by the personal eccentricity of the witnesses.

News of the massacre filtered out to an unbelieving world for days and weeks after the fact through reporters and eyewitnesses. Although denied at first by the Salvadoran and US governments, the news of the massacre was instrumental in exposing the atrocities and abuses by the Salvadoran military. A landmark human rights case began as a result. This was a clear case of the truth needing to be told.

The purported sole survivor of the El Mozote massacre was an articulate young woman named Rufina. Her account was very descriptive and informative, with complete details of the events leading up to the massacre, as well as details of the massacre itself. She personally witnessed the death of her husband and her children, along with hundreds of others. Her story captivated thousands and was instrumental in getting the news out, "So this never happens again!"

The El Mozote massacre became the life work of Rufina as she told her story to ever growing numbers of visitors and groups arriving to the site. She began to charge for her services because she could not dedicate full time to the cause without some compensation.

It soon became a pilgrimage atmosphere that went far beyond the sharing of the testimony and actually took on religious overtones. Rufina began wearing a green robe embroidered with Christian symbols, holding candle-lit services and blessing water brought by the pilgrims. Her strong eyewitness testimony was gradually replaced by her priestess role.

Her story, perhaps suffering from too much repetition, began to evolve. Rufina's own role in the story gradually became more protagonist, more central and much more than a simple eyewitness.

Rufina died in 2007, and at her request is buried at the monument to the massacre victims in El Mozote. Movements are well underway to place Rufina among the martyrs and heroes of the Salvadoran Revolution.

One of Rufina's daughters is the embodiment of hope; the new birth springing up after tragedy. Born several years after the massacre, she brought new life to Rufina, who, according to her account, had lost all of her children at El Mozote on that fateful day. The daughter is in a university now. Scholarships and support guarantee her education and livelihood.

The irony was not lost on the older daughter who should actually have been one of the El Mozote dead. Fidelia was largely ignored because she did not fit into the story. Actually, she had joined the guerrilla forces and was part of a combat unit at the time of the massacre. As such, she was swept into the background and did not enjoy the benefits of her mother's livelihood.

Fidelia got by the best she could, many thought the easiest way she could. She provided the services of town courtesan, a trade she apparently picked up during a brief period in the US, while struggling to find opportunity as an illegal immigrant.

Upon her mother's death, Fidelia converted her home into a museum in honor of Rufina. Many wondered if this was out of dedication or opportunism. *Whichever the case, she worked tirelessly for her mother's memory until her own death in March of 2012.*

I had several interesting and very frank conversations with Fidelia during her last three years, a catharsis of sorts on her part. My sense is that she genuinely desired to become that which she was projecting.

Many found Rufina's conversion of a tragedy into a livelihood somewhat disconcerting. The evolution of her testimony even led to speculation regarding veracity, and if in fact she was present that tragic December day in Mozote. Her obsession in being the sole survivor focused attention on herself, but actually weakened her testimony.

There were in fact two other survivors from El Mozote itself, and another young woman who survived the massacre at La Joya, which occurred during the same military operation. Eyewitness accounts have come from local men forced to serve as guides for the military on that fateful day and even by one or more of the soldiers involved. These testimonies add weight to and corroborate Rufina's account.

There are other eyewitnesses out there who may come forward someday, perhaps maybe even one of the ten foreign military advisors assigned to the Atlacatl Battalion, during that time period.

The truth and fact of the massacre stands on its own. Brought to light by courageous testimony and then withstanding even the twisting of that same testimony to serve personal interests.

A cause to pause: do all legends begin this way? The story teller becoming larger than the story itself? Embellishment only serves to distract, it seems.

I came to know of the massacre in a different way. I was an aid worker in the Salvadoran refugee camp at Colomoncagua, Honduras, when on October 22 of 1984, word came over the Radio Venceremos that Colonel Monterossa, the military commander responsible for the massacre, had been killed by a booby trap he had taken on his helicopter.

The camp went wild with celebration. It was one of the few times I saw so much joy in so many faces. All work halted, hugs all around, music and dancing started early and ended late into the night.

The story of El Mozote was repeated to me dozens of times that night, over endless cups of coffee and corn bread.

The joy continued for weeks, as the girls in the camps were sporting new string necklaces sent over by their boyfriends from the combat zone. The pendants were carved as birds and hearts, all cut out of the aluminum fuselage of Colonel Monterossa's helicopter.

Guerrilla Tourism

In 1987 I started working with communities well within the war zone in the northern provinces of San Miguel and Morazán. By then, human rights had become an important issue and were taken into account by the government and the guerrillas when planning military actions. Actually the guerrillas, in general, had been more careful to not abuse the civilian population and the government army was playing catch-up.

Civilians were now allowed to return to their homes within the conflict areas and the international community had been asked to assist in the repopulation effort.

Persuading organizations to give assistance to returning communities in the north-east was difficult. The guerrilla forces of the ERP had the reputation of being a very militaristic group that could win stand-up military battles like no one else but basically had no public relations effort. This was in stark contrast to the FPL in Chalatenango and the FAL in Guazapa, which had developed long-term relationships with community organizations, solidarity groups and international organizations.

Work within the combat zone, of course, required coordination with the guerrillas. They were the de facto authority and civilians returning to their territory added new responsibilities and concerns to their ongoing activities. One expressed concern of the ERP was the lack of social and civilian organizations within their areas of control.

They were already anticipating an end to the armed conflict and therefore desired strong civilian organizations that would lead the social and economic development of the growing communities. The lack of local organizations would leave the population completely dependent on the disposition and availability of outside assistance. The short term need for these new civilian organizations would be the programming of emergency subsistence aid, as well as human rights monitoring.

In a series of meetings with several ERP commanders, which took place in Torola and Perquín, I was requested to assist with the building of the needed civilian organizations within the conflict zone. Furthermore, I was asked to help those new organizations get a foot in the door with the international cooperation.

Understanding the reluctance of international organizations to support work in areas under ERP control, I played the one card that would always draw them in, an interview with the guerrillas. So, one by one I would take international representatives out to meet the guerrillas, or the Belgian priest who was working in the war zone.

Getting in and out of a war zone is not as difficult as it may seem. It's all about timing. Generally it meant getting an early start and passing the fixed military checkpoints before daybreak. When running late a few mornings, we drove by soldiers out brushing their teeth and combing their hair before getting down to the task of closing the road.

Once through the checkpoints, it was a twenty minute drive to the river. The Torola River was the natural dividing line between government held territory and the guerrilla stronghold.

During rainy season, with the river running high, there was no safe retreat route for invading government forces. If a complete rout occurred, the river would claim as many drowning victims as casualties from guerrilla fire. Except for an occasional large scale campaign of three to four thousand troops, the war zone of Morazán was generally calmer than the capital city, San Salvador. Days could go by without a shot being fired.

There were several options for crossing the river, depending on the entry point. At Carolina, there was a little homemade flat bottom boat; they called it a barge, attached to a cable to keep it from being swept downstream. During dry season the river could be forded there. I drove an old Landcruiser, with a little diesel engine that did not mind running underwater at times.

The San Simon entry was a bit different. The crossing was a pool called *The Witch*, a deep, treacherous hole, with a strong undercurrent. Locals said that those who got pulled under never came back up. Crossing there had to be coordinated with people on the other side of the river. They tossed a rope and visitors were unceremoniously dragged to the other side.

The only practical way to keep clothing and shoes dry for the four hour uphill climb to follow, was to put everything in a big plastic bag which was hauled over first.

Describing it as extremely vulnerable is an understatement for the feeling experienced standing out in the open, on a big rock in the middle of a raging river, in an active war zone. Just standing there all alone, in your skivvies… waiting for that stupid rope to be thrown back.

The Devil Himself in my sights

Zipping through the Colonia Roma while heading to the University of Central America (UCA), I came around the curve and found the Devil Himself lined up right between the headlights of my Toyota Landcrusier.

I was driving at about forty-five miles an hour. Roberto D'Abuisson, the leader of the violent hard right and the architect of the infamous Salvadoran death squads, stood all alone in the middle of the street about sixty feet away.

And time slowed down, way down and almost ground to a halt.

I had all the time in the world to make the right decision.

I knew instantly that I could get away with it. I knew where to ditch the Jeep and how to be out of the country within four hours.

This man was personally responsible for the pain and suffering of people I had grown to love. He was the icon of everything on the wrong side of the war, the essence of evil itself.

My personal convictions, hard to separate from my up-bringing, clashed with the ideal of laying down my life for my brother. Make the ultimate sacrifice and go to hell for it. What greater sacrifice than losing your soul to do a good deed?

Will this help the cause? Will this stop the war? Why do I have this decision laid on my shoulders?

D'Abuisson was laughing at someone across the street. Suddenly he went sober, turned his head and looked me in the eye.

Nothing magical about him, so normal, even a bit smaller in real life. I drove by.

I went straight home. That sickening emotion that grips the gut, like when I killed my first deer, hit me and I relived the drive, again and again. Maybe I should have done it.

Did values or fear hold me back?

I have no idea.

The fact that D'Abuisson, several years later and on his deathbed, forced a reluctant right to the negotiation table to sign the peace accords is valuable hindsight. The thought that his untimely death could have prolonged the conflict chills me to the bone.

Destiny. When do we control it? And when do we let it control us? And why can't we have all the information when we need it?

Watching my Shadow Stride on

Working with the communities in northern San Miguel was made a lot easier with support by the Catholic parish in Ciudad Barrios. Father V and the sisters there were very accommodating, giving me a place to sleep in the convent, good food and company.

It was a good place to leave my Jeep when I would be going *into the zone* for several days at a time, rather than leave it abandoned down by the river.

Father V, like many of the Catholic priests near conflictive areas, had a fine line to walk. Their flock came from both sides of *the line* and many congregations could be split down the middle politically. The local military authorities always suspected them to be guerrilla sympathizers. At the same time, they also had to maintain a good relationship with the insurgency. The arrival of an international organization to assist with the communities on *the other side* strengthened Father V's position in this balance. So he was happy to have the help.

He would drive me up to the river crossing. "If anything happens, just say you're working with the parish," was his advice, as he saw me off.

On one of these trips, into the second day, we got word that the Third Brigade was on its way. It was decision time! The guerrilla commander in the area called me over and laid out the options. Two actually: either stay in the community or go with them. I had four hours to decide.

The option of trying to get out on my own was rejected immediately as too dangerous. To go with the guerrillas was a long term decision.

Someone in the community would inform and I would be unable to go back as a civilian.

No one knew what would happen if I just stayed in the community. It hadn't been tried before.

Because we were trying to open the area for international support and presence I decided to stay with the community and see what would happen. I did move down from where I had been staying, to the community of San Diego, close to the river and right at the entry point of the military incursion.

As the first lines of troops went by I was in plain sight in a hammock, pretending to read a bible handed to me by the lady of the house. After about ten minutes, one of the soldiers noticed me and I was taken into custody. An officer asked what I was doing there, who I was with and did I have military permission. I answered all of his questions clearly and tried to be very matter-of-fact. He spent more time on the radio asking what to do with me than actually talking with me.

After several hours, it was decided that I would be flown by helicopter to the High Command in San Salvador for interrogation. The troops were on the move, so I had to go with them until the helicopter arrived. I was taken to a clearing close to where I had started out the day where we waited, and waited. Darkness fell. Finally I was told that the copter could not arrive until the next day and that we would go back to where they found me to spend the night.

I was not particularly worried about my personal safety. This was the Third Brigade, not one of the crazy outfits, and the fact that a Swiss national had been killed some ten days earlier meant that the military had to be more careful for a while.

Unknown to me at the time, a couple of community members got out, hired a truck and went straight to Father V with the news of my capture. He was speaking with military authorities on my behalf, within hours. The guerrillas also sent word by radio to their diplomatic representatives in Mexico, who alerted the human rights organizations.

Walking with soldiers at night, deep in guerrilla territory is not pleasant. When I was told to please go first, it was not an act of courtesy. I was the point man, the shield for safe passage on this night-time excursion.

The group of some twenty soldiers stayed about forty feet behind me while shining two flashlights on my back. Watching my shadow stride ahead of me gave me something to focus on during the forty minute walk. I was sure no land mines would be out and that the guerrillas would not be ambushing us, but the soldiers were very nervous. So I also kept track of where I could dive over the embankment if something went wrong.

Finally, back in the community of San Diego, I was told that I would have to stay with them for the night. I asked if I was captured or just taken in for questioning.

"Oh no," they replied as if to reassure me, "if you were captured you would have your hands tied and a bag over your head."

"Ok," I said, "then I'll stay in this house and you can call me in the morning when you're ready to go."

I turned and went into the house as if we had reached an agreement. They settled in for the night around the house.

In the early morning hours, as the lady of the house started the fire to make coffee, I burned all the notes and letters I had brought along for the Belgian priest and others working in the war zone.

Later that morning I was taken across the river to the soccer field in Carolina to wait for the helicopter. It was a Huey, filled to capacity with troops. My spot was sitting on the floor with my feet dangling out and two knees on my back. As we headed out over the town cemetery it took so long to gain altitude that I couldn't help thinking how easy it would be to shoot us down.

After a twenty minute flight we arrived at the Third Brigade in San Miguel. I had not been pushed out but someone had changed the plan from San Salvador to San Miguel. After several hours of waiting, I had a little interview with Colonel Ponce. He lectured me about going where I shouldn't go, and then I was free to leave.

I walked out the front gate and caught the next bus to San Salvador, shaking.

In an ironic twist, I would visit the Third Brigade years later because three of my children were born there. Due to the lack of health facilities in San Miguel, the maternal care section of the Social Security Hospital is located within the Third Brigade, where wounded soldiers were once treated.

Care to Dance?

While visiting a repatriated community near the Lempa River in central San Miguel, I was invited to a party.

It was a small settlement, deep in the territory controlled by the guerrilla forces of the RN. We were assisting the community with seeds for subsistence farming, some emergency aid and an international presence as a deterrent to abuses by the military.

Preparation for the party started early in the afternoon, with the women cooking *tamales* and the old guys tuning up the fiddle, guitar and bass. A relaxed joyful atmosphere set in. It was always a pleasure to come to this community and stay a few days. The people were very cooperative and friendly and always took the time to tell stories and share experiences.

Just before dusk, we headed off in a procession carrying the food and musical instruments. We went to a clearing, toward the river, about fifteen minutes away. Our walk accompanied by a beautiful sunset. Firewood was gathered for a bonfire and the food was put out.

I was just starting to wonder why we had come here rather than have a party back in the community, when a column of carriers walked in.

Seventy-five strong, and the fittest group of guerrillas I had ever seen, carriers were the young men that transported weapons shipments from the coast into the mountains on the northern border of El Salvador. With legs like NFL football players and outfitted with good hiking boots, these guys walked in with a spring in their step that only occurs when you unload a heavy pack, and are ready to dance.

The small contingency of armed guerrillas along as an escort took turns at perimeter guard duty and enjoying the party.

Caught up in the spirit of the party, I came up to one of the women on the escort team.

"Care to dance?" I asked.

She turned and looked me straight in the eyes, "If I weren't a guerrilla, you'd never ask me to dance," she stated as she kept her gaze steady and harsh.

I was left with my mouth open, as she haughtily turned her attention back to the festivities.

She was right, of course, because she was one of the most unattractive women I've ever run across. I slouched off and sat with the old guys for the remainder of the night.

Fitting into the Community

For a while I lived in a middle-class residential neighborhood in San Salvador. Miravalle was home to professionals and office worker types who were all very prim and proper. Not a lot of contact with neighbors, but enough prying eyes peeping out of windows to require keeping a somewhat *decent* appearance.

At the time I was working with some of the communities in southern San Miguel and Usulután. One of their main difficulties was getting access to medicine. First, it was difficult to simply get their hands on it and second, it was difficult to get it through the military checkpoints. I was able to get the basic general health medication they needed, but they didn't want me to transport it.

“Much too risky,” they said, “we'll handle that.”

After the first two visitors came to my house to take shipments back, I voiced my concern that the women they sent stood out too much.

“Look at the neighborhood,” I said, “Can they dress up a little and fit in with everyone else here?”

“Sure, no problem,” was the reply.

A week later, my doorbell rang. I opened the garage door to a plumpish eighteen year old girl wearing a tight yellow top with a short purple skirt that almost reached her black stockings, topped off with red shoes.

“How do I look?” she shyly asked as she tugged at her skirt.

Speechless, I waved her in. “Perfect, you look perfect,” I was finally able to say.

What else could I say? So I made sure she was there for almost an hour before heading off with the package. Had to keep up appearances you know.

It did fit in well with the neighborhood, if there been any doubt before. The regular routine of a call girl for a couple of hours each week probably made everyone more comfortable.

The Offensive of 89

The guerrilla offensive of November 11, 1989, was one of those secrets everyone knew about. Two days prior saw the supermarkets emptied of all nonperishable food.

When my live-in maid disappeared on the afternoon of the 10th, I had my suspicions. So when I saw her a few days later on the front lines, armed with an AKA, I didn't admonish her about leaving dirty dishes in the sink.

In the middle of the night I was awoken by loud explosions and gunfire. As I watched out of my bedroom window, the whole north side of the city lit up with a full scale battle. Almost instantly, a DC3 gunship was circling overhead pouring fire down on the National University.

Years later, the American crew of that gunship would be demanding recognition for combat service in El Salvador, but that's another story.

The next morning I was out bright and early, standing on a street corner in the community of Zacamil, just north of the National University, wearing a white shirt and waving a makeshift white flag.

Most of the gunfire and the occasional tank round was toward the east with a little scattered fire five or six blocks to the west. Zacamil was deadly quiet. Nothing was moving and no one was in sight.

Just me out on the corner with a stupid little white flag.

The battle the night before had been at defensive positions on the northern flank of the city as the guerrillas advanced down from the volcano and took up positions within the residential areas.

The guerrilla strategy was not a direct military victory so they did not attack military installations. Their plan was to take over and hold large portions of the city. Territorial control of urban areas and popular support would cause a stalemate which would require a cease-fire and force negotiations.

The morning after was fairly quiet because the military, expecting an eminent attack on their installations had drawn back into defensive positions, rather than facing down the incoming columns of guerrillas in the streets.

I had been asked by the ERP weeks earlier to show up at this street corner, "once the offensive begins." While never privy to military plans, I was told what to expect regarding the stalemate and cease-fire and was requested to be ready to set up an emergency attention center for the needs of the community. It was a continuation of what I had been doing in San

Miguel and Morazán. That was to assist civilian populations inside guerrilla held territory, only this time the territory did not yet exist.

So, there I was, standing on the street corner, waving my silly little flag, wondering if I'm supposed to go out and look for these guys or what.

I was about ready to leave when a column of guerrillas came strolling down the center of the street. Chiquito (little boy) and Chicón (big boy), two of the ERP commanders, were at the lead. Chiquito was taking two strides for each one of Chicón's, adding comic relief to the whole affair.

They made fun of my flag and jokingly offered to trade it for an AKA.

I replied, "Maybe later, let's see how you guys do first."

They told me they had run into some resistance in Montebello which threw them a little off schedule, then excused themselves as they had a territory to take over.

I was asked to go back several blocks in the direction they were coming from to find a couple of wounded guerrillas. They had left them in a house with civilians and wanted me to see if I could work out a way to evacuate them.

"Better go right away," they said, "The soldiers will probably be closing in behind us soon."

"This is great," I mumbled to myself, as I walked the four blocks into no-man's land, "First day on the job, and I get sent out between the lines."

As I approached the house they had indicated, shots rang out. They were small caliber buzzes, zipping by several feet away. I hit the ground behind a small embankment, grumbling, "Don't these guys know I'm here to help them?"

Luckily they weren't good shots and had been left with only pistols. I couldn't see any point in shouting that I was there to help and was a little concerned with the gunfire approaching from the north, so I got out.

I went back and told Chiquito that I had tried and that maybe the next time there could be a little communication that help was on the way.

I have no idea of the fate of those two wounded men. They may have melted back into the population. They may have been captured or perhaps were assisted by one of the paramedic organizations.

The conflict in El Salvador saw a proliferation of volunteer paramedic organizations such as the Green Cross, the Blue Cross, the "Commandos of Salvamento." There were at least eight different colors and brands.

Extremely brave and without much thought to personal safety, these volunteers were the first responders to all man-made and natural disasters. They would burrow under earthquake rubble to pull out survivors long before the *experts* arrived. Stretcher bearers dodging bullets to get to the wounded, physically sheltering civilians while evacuating battle zones, the volunteers in these organizations were true selfless heroes.

By the time I got back to the zone in the afternoon of that first day, the army had already been probing the guerrilla defenses in Zacamil, resulting in sporadic fire fights. I left my Jeep in a quiet area and walked down the long sloping street and across the bridge over the ravine which more or less defined the zone. Once in, I had to cross through one of the temporary earthquake settlements. I was headed for a three-story apartment complex that had been taken over by the guerrillas.

A smattering of gunfire scattered the civilians who had come out on the street during the lull. On my left, a young man came staggering out of a latrine and collapsed to the ground.

The bystanders mistook me for a doctor and I could not convince them otherwise. They insisted that I do something to save the guy, he had only just fallen over. I could not find a pulse and it took a little while to find the wound although he was wearing white pants. There was a pencil sized entry hole in the thigh, next to the groin. It was a small caliber, probably from an M16, but had severed the femoral artery, causing massive internal bleeding. There was nothing to do but help carry him inside, to where the neighbors were already arriving with flowers and candles for the wake.

As I continued through makeshift paths between the shacks, the fighting broke out in earnest. I had to take refuge in a shallow drainage ditch. The door of the shack on my right opened and a lady waved me inside. Gratefully, I accepted the invitation and rolled in.

It was home to an older couple, their daughter and her two children. A temporary shelter like the rest of the community, it was a simple pine structure with tin roofing and siding, with a dirt floor. I wondered if it was one of the shelters that we had provided materials for. The family had settled in the best they could with an aluminum/vinyl dining set, a television, a couple of beds and a little propane cooktop.

A surreal scene unfolded as the automatic hospitality of the Salvadoran poor kicked in. "Please have a seat," as I was offered a chair. Introductions were made all around and I accepted the coffee kindly put forth. The two children were on one of the beds and the rest of us sitting properly in a circle, chatting normal small-talk.

We talked of the battle raging around us as if it were the weather. The man pointed out the bullet holes in the roof that would have to be repaired. The conversation would lull when the fire-fight intensified outside or when a sharp splat added another hole in the siding and then would pick up as the fighting died down.

I noticed they had a little shop in the house, a common neighborhood store with a few basic items for sale. I bought a pack of cigarettes and told the lady to keep the change. She, however, insisted on searching through the drawer and a few cans on the shelf to find the exact change. Each one solemnly accepted the offered cigarette and we sat smoking in silence until the fighting calmed down.

When I finally made it into the command post on the second floor of the third line of the apartment buildings, Chiquito was facing another problem. His troops had not eaten in two days and they were not getting the support from the civilians they had expected. He was at the point of ordering a requisition team to go out and take what they needed but did not want to antagonize the civilian population. They also had not brought along transistor radios, only military gear, and had no access to the news.

"You guys really think ahead," I mumbled as I handed over the radio I had been carrying to keep track of the news myself. I also dipped into the reserve I had been carrying around for emergencies and told him to buy what he needed.

"No sense in creating more enemies if you already have your hands full."

The FMLN miscalculated popular response to the offensive. Just ten years earlier, social organizations could put two to three hundred thousand people in the streets for the cause. So the thought was that with a show of force in urban areas, a large spontaneous civilian support would take hold.

In those ten years various factors came into play which lowered an active popular support considerably. First, those with a predisposition to join in the armed struggle had already joined guerrilla organizations and many had died or were disabled as a result. Second, many of the fiery street protestors of old had become professionals or had a decent job and had started families. Now they had something to lose. Third, the composition of the popular neighborhoods had changed. Much of the population was now made up of those fleeing the war in rural areas and they just wanted to stay out of harm's way.

Indeed, much of the urban population was ideologically or politically aligned with the left, but that did not translate to direct action such as taking up arms.

In the early morning hours of November 16, the Atlacatl battalion entered the Jesuit Central American University and assassinated six Jesuit priests, their housekeeper and her daughter. It was an act of desperation, and perhaps revenge. The Salvadoran military was close to collapse.

Aerial bombing of urban areas began, and the nicety of being careful of the civilian population was set aside for the need to root out the guerrilla forces before it became too late.

Entry into Zacamil became more difficult. Grenades were being tossed out of passing helicopters, along with the rocket attacks and general strafing. A new weapon was employed on apartment complexes. Balls of burning white flames were dropped from helicopters. They would burn straight through the roof and set everything inside on fire.

The first six days were difficult and the sudden escalation to total war became overbearing. Several of the aid workers who had known the Jesuit priests well and had ongoing work within the communities under attack, went into emotional shock and had to be evacuated.

As I came out of the Camino Real about midmorning on the seventh day of the offensive, I ran across the gentleman who had shared his shelter with me on the first day. It was where we had sat so calmly while the bullets flew overhead. He was standing on the corner in front of the hotel, holding the television in his arms and had tears streaming down his face.

"It's all gone, it's all gone," he repeated over and over.

I could get no response to my questions about his family or as to what happened. I cannot be sure he even noticed me.

At loss as to how to help, I left him standing there. Tears streaming down his face.

As the civilian population became increasingly affected by the escalation of firepower, the FMLN made the decision to pull out. They had obtained part of their goal. They had fought the army to a standstill in San Salvador and San Miguel. They did not get the active popular support they expected and had not obtained the cease-fire they desired. But continuing would achieve only more loss of life.

I slipped back into the apartments one last time. The shanty town was burned out and abandoned. Barricades of shot-up cars and trucks blocked the street in front of the apartments.

It was deadly quiet. The only sound was the echo of my footsteps walking in. The guerrillas had left overnight and the soldiers had not yet arrived.

It was eerie, too silent and smelled of death.

I turned and walked softly out.

Seals to the Rescue?

As the bombardment of popular communities continued, several units of the ERP and FPL pulled out and, in a lightning strike, took over the affluent Escalón and San Benito neighborhoods. Of course the Salvadoran Air Force would not bomb that side of town.

On November 21, Chicón and a group of commandos took over the Sheraton Hotel in Escalón. Among the guests were several diplomats and the General Secretary of the Organization of American States, Joao Baena Soarez. Unknown to the guerrillas was the fact that a group of American advisors were also staying at the hotel. Reports put the number at twelve. They blockaded themselves on an upper floor and refused to accept the idea that the guerrillas were not at all interested in them.

Twenty-eight hours later, the guerrillas slipped away. Their point had been made. Army Special Forces were preparing an attack and they saw no reason to put the diplomats at risk.

On the afternoon of the twenty second, while driving home, I was passed by a military convoy. The convoy consisted of three unmarked vehicles, two trucks and a semi with flatbed trailer.

The flatbed carried tarp covered equipment with four skin-headed white guys sitting on top, weapons pointing in all directions.

I guess a team had been brought in for the emergency. I was glad it was a dry run.

One Page at a Time

The Camino Real Hotel became the headquarters and dormitory for international aid workers during the offensive of 1989. The press corps had taken over the second floor, so it was considered the safest place to be. I stayed for a few nights myself, but generally just stopped by to catch up on news and coordinate work.

As I came in one afternoon, I noticed the aid workers gathered in tight groups and talking in worried hushed tones. It turns out that J, one of the group, had been captured by the military, because of weapons supposedly found in her house.

At first everyone was worried about her personal safety, but that soon became worry about being associated with her. Suddenly, someone remembered that she had been staying at the hotel and that all of her stuff was in one of the rooms. At that point, everyone who was staying with her ran upstairs, got their own things, and left J's belongings in an otherwise empty room.

Fear was obviously gripping the group but dumping J's stuff in the trash was not an ideal solution, so I volunteered to take care of it. I sorted her clothes, packed up the computer and printer and filled four oversized plastic garbage bags with notebooks, letters and assorted documents.

As I prepared to leave, D, the leader of J's organization, politely offered to take care of the computer and printer, probably to lighten my load.

No one would touch anything else or lend a hand, so I got a busboy to get a dolly and take the bags out to my Jeep.

Back in my living room, I sat on the floor looking at four garbage bags full of papers and asked myself what I was going to do. It was probably not the safest place to have this stuff and I already had enough to be careful about.

What if these papers were found and there was something there that would incriminate her? I decided to go through the bags and see what there was.

The first time through took several hours. I separated everything into stacks of personal notes, letters, newspaper articles and propaganda. I burned the articles and political propaganda. The stacks were now reduced by half.

When J did not get out right away and the government announced they were building the case against her, I made the second selection. This time around called for much more time. I went through her mail, including a bunch of unopened envelopes, carefully noting the amount of cash and personal checks in each one.

Then I started to go through the notebooks. As soon as I started, I knew I was in trouble. She had written down every thought that came into her head. I was embarrassed. It was like walking into her room at the wrong time, "Oops, sorry."

Thinking that if the aid workers were worried about their association with her, then perhaps the organizations and persons in the correspondence would be also, I burned the letters. As an afterthought I burned the checks too.

J was sent to prison at the women's detention center in Ilopango, if memory serves me correctly. It was a bit of a scandal. It became a high profile case with a US congressman involved, with a potential long prison sentence among other things.

All the while, I had those notebooks stored away and I was starting to worry. Since I was already walking a fine line, pretty close to the edge, I decided to go ahead and check out the notebooks.

I have never encountered such honesty in written word. Her soul was bared and I was violating her intimacy for such a coarse and practical, perhaps even superficial, purpose.

Nothing in her writings would have implicated her directly in the activity she was accused of.

But our thoughts, our deepest thoughts, go much further than our actions, don't they?

Don't even bother asking me for details. My memory went up in the black smoke of each page I burned. One by one I burned them.

I still wonder what took longer: for her to put the thoughts down or for me to finally decide to destroy them.

I met J on a street corner in Washington years later. I awkwardly handed her an envelope with perhaps three torn pages that remained. She sat down on the curb, and cried and cried.

I don't know if she has, or will, forgive me. I wonder if I deserve it.

Nonchalant Bravery

Women made up approximately thirty-five percent of the guerrilla forces. They were not relegated to the back lines and many were full-fledged combatants. During my many trips to the war zones I was always impressed by the casualness displayed by these women. It was as if toting a gun and routing out enemy soldiers was a natural thing for a woman to be doing.

During the offensive of 1989, I witnessed many examples of their bravery. Two stand out in my mind as examples of the level of nonchalance shown under fire.

One afternoon while at home catching a shower and a change of clothes, bullets from a helicopter began to rain down on the street in front of the house. I lived on the south side of town, which was fairly quiet for the first few days of the offensive. Helicopters had been firing rockets into the coffee plantations on the surrounding hills for a day or so, but the gunfire was new.

Looking out the window, I noticed a young girl, who could not have been more than fifteen, leaning against the electric post on the other side of the street. She was almost overweighed by the AKA tucked under her arm. As the copter circled, firing, she simply circled the post as well. She was the only person in sight, seemingly all alone on the street.

The final attack by the copter was overwhelming. I headed for cover under the stairwell because it was just a bit too close for comfort. *My next-door neighbor suffered a head wound during the attack, as the hail of bullets rained down through his roof.* As the copter flew away, I rushed back to the window to see the damage. The dust was still rising for a moment and then it cleared. There she was, as if nothing had happened, back out on the corner, the AKA tucked under her arm.

The second example occurred as I was coming out of the Zacamil zone one night. It was already dark and much too late for comfort. I had started out on time but a cowboy soldier, in a rubber-tired tank, had made a mad dash through the street in front of the guerrilla line and escaped through the shanty town that was my entry and exit point.

I was about a half block away when the tank came roaring around the corner, firing in all directions. I made a record-breaking fifty-yard dash, cleared an embankment with a fence in one bound and rolled into a house as the door was closing.

By the time it was safe to leave, darkness had fallen. As I walked up the hill to the neutral zone where my Jeep was parked, I noticed a pile of burlap sacks on the sidewalk. I had come across a munitions delivery for the guerrillas in Zacamil. At first I thought it had been abandoned after the tank ran through. Then I noticed a small shape stepping forward as if to keep me at a distance. A young girl, not more than thirteen years old, was bravely standing guard over the supplies.

"Good night," I said as I passed by.

"Que le vaya bien, *May you go well,*" she replied with a shy smile.

I watched from the shadows about half a block away until other dark shapes arrived to carry the sacks away.

Real Fear

Several days into the offensive, I decided to try to find one of the secretaries who worked at the office. We had not seen her since the beginning of the offensive and I wanted to make sure she and her family were alright.

There was a lull in the fighting around midday, so I set off, with my ever present white flag, on the six block walk to her neighborhood. It was quiet. It was warm with no breeze. A handful of civilians were taking advantage of the lull to look for water and food or to move to a safer area.

While passing the old Zacamil movie theatre, an angry hornet like buzz passed my ear and splattered against the curb. I crouched and waddled to an embankment ahead. As I fought down the terror, I had my first real whiff of fear. It was an indescribable acrid smell rising off my body, like really bad body odor with bile and acid thrown in.

It is one thing to be bouncing around on the outskirts of a fire-fight, but it is completely different knowing you are the target of a sniper.

I gathered my wits and courage and took stock of the situation. It seemed best not to go forward into unknown territory. That might give the guy a better angle. I decided to wait for a few minutes and then head back. When a small group of civilians walked by, I stood up and walked back to safety with them.

Several hours later, miffed at myself for giving up so easily, I decided to have another shot at getting to the secretary's house. Again I headed out with my little white flag, and this time I was going to gut it out.

As I passed the movie theatre again, a movement on the left caught my eye. Looking around, I saw the alley next to the theatre was packed with National Guard crawling in close formation on their elbows and knees, with their G3s held at firing position. They were about halfway down the alley, advancing at a slow but steady pace.

I kept my own pace but started thinking fast. Should I go forward or go back? I had no idea what lay ahead. If this column had backup or an armored division, it would come from that direction.

Figuring I probably had just enough time to return to the *neutral zone*, I continued another half block then turned around and started the trek back to the shanty town and to safety. Fixing my gaze on the tin shacks some three blocks in the distance, I causally walked as quickly as possible, not breaking into a run but trying not to look like those goofy Olympic walkers.

As I passed the alley, I kept my gaze straight ahead, counting my steps to keep my mind busy, with the acrid odor of fear starting to rise again.

As I passed in front of the apartment blocks, I noticed several guerrillas lounging on the second floor balcony. They seemed to not have a care in the world. I recognized the university student who waved. He was just a kid and had been in my office several times, looking for support for student organizing.

Maintaining my pace and keeping my hands in front of my body, I franticly tried to signal that an attack was coming.

I think he understood. I hope he understood.

He died that day.

I don't know if in that attack or another.

The Numbers Game

In all probability, negotiations would have been put off for one more shot at the military option if either side had known how weak their enemy was.

Fatigue was taking its toll on the ranks of the FMLN during the last years of the war. New recruits were harder and harder to find. Recruiting from the second and even third generation of the original combatants was beginning to meet resistance as mothers refused to let their remaining children join the ranks. Had they not given enough with the one, two or more sons and daughters sacrificed for the revolution?

The military had a different kind of problem. Corruption had risen to levels that, as evidenced during the guerrilla offensive of 1989, endangered the very survival of the Armed Forces. The colonel in each brigade was administratively responsible for the recruitment, training, clothing, feeding and arming of his troops. When the High Command called in reinforcements during the offensive, they ordered up entire divisions of phantom troops. They only existed in the budget and expenditures reports.

Actual troops were stretched so thin that a diversionary feint against the High Command in San Salvador practically took the Command Headquarters. It probably would have if the guerrillas not fallen back as planned when their mission was completed.

By early 1991, negotiations had progressed to the point that the FMLN needed to begin planning for the demobilization of troops and the programs necessary for their transition and incorporation into civilian life.

The ERP requested that I assist them in the process. I helped them develop a complete census questionnaire. There were over four hundred blanks to fill in with information on troop levels, operational budgets, educational levels, health, material resources, infrastructure, options for economic development and social assistance needs in the communities. I went to each of the eleven operational zones to explain the mechanics of the census and by August we had compiled results to begin planning the reinsertion programs.

I was entrusted with the number of guerrilla troops by zone, sex, age group, responsibility and time of service, plus a lot of other data, during the war. It was a little nerve-racking, there were a lot of people around who would have gone to great pains to get those numbers, but the information was necessary to avoid the huge social problem of not being prepared for demobilizing guerrilla fighters.

The numbers used at the negotiation table were much higher, of course. The FMLN needed the threat of a large guerrilla force to bargain for conditions and obtain concessions from the government negotiators. This actually did create another dilemma.

As the cease fire agreement approached, the guerrilla forces practically doubled overnights with new recruits for what was jokingly referred to as *The Army of Presentation.*

Negotiation

Negotiations resulting in a lasting agreement happen only when the extremes are sitting at the table. A lukewarm or middle ground stance does not have the real power required to reach an agreement.

The Salvadoran peace process began early on in the conflict, with several clear opportunities for reaching settlement. Those opportunities, however, held no interest for the protagonists involved, nor for their Cold War backers.

By 1984, the situation could best be described as two regular armies at a standoff, both holding territory with permanent defensive positions from which they launched attacks against the other. Both were gaining experience, capacity and support.

Within this context Jose Napoleon Duarte of the Christian Democratic Party, is elected as President of El Salvador. A landmark event, Duarte is the first civilian president in the history of the country, creating a high level of expectation that a middle ground position of power could bring an end to the conflict.

The Christian Democrats initiated a series of social reforms and began to explore the possibility of a negotiated end to the conflict. The first face-to-face dialogue took place in October of 1984, in the town of La Palma in Chalatenango. I was fortunate enough to be among the crowd of several thousand who were allowed past the military checkpoints to witness the event. The FDR (political arm of the FMLN) spokesperson and the guerrilla commanders who addressed the crowd sounded hopeful that the dialogue would lead to an ending of the war in the not too distant future.

The Christian Democrats (PDC), however, did not hold the reins of real power. They did not represent the powerful interests that fueled the conflict in the first place. Roberto D'Abuisson, the charismatic leader of the hard right, used a graphic television ad during the election to air his view of the PDC, whose party colors were green.

"The Christian Democrats are like a watermelon", he stated, standing before a table with a watermelon sitting in the middle. Then slashing it open with a machete, he would continue, "Green on the outside, red on the inside".

This was the same format D'Abuisson had used to identify subversives. He would run a television ad naming a group as communist and show photos of the leaders. Once identified, two options were available. They could flee or die at the hands of the death squads.

The Reagan administration used the PDC as an excuse to increase military aid to El Salvador. They basically ignored the objections based on human rights and corruption concerns, while accepting the concept that the democratically-elected government was under attack by communist aggression. The niceties involved were not particularly important.

Further attempts at dialogue were not fruitful at the time. I was visiting in El Salvador when another round of talks was to be held in Zaragoza, south of the capital. It was called off at the last moment leaving thousands of us waiting in the road with tanks and armored personnel carriers constantly driving by, weapons menacingly pointed at the crowd.

A new hope sprang up with the Central American Presidents' Esquipulas II declaration, of August 1987. This declaration was the culmination of efforts by Costa Rican president Oscar Aries, who would later win the Nobel Peace Prize, and covered procedures to arrive at a firm and lasting peace in Central America.

President Duarte offered amnesty and unconditional peace talks to the guerrilla forces, and on October 5, negotiations resumed at the Papal Nuncio in San Salvador.

An atmosphere of hope surrounded these talks. It was palatable, tangible and filled with expectation. Tens of thousands gathered in a vacant block close to the negotiation site. Thousands of red FMLN flags were waving, revolutionary music played at full blast. There was a group excitement impossible to resist. Popular slogans were voiced in a roaring chant, right into the face of the oppressors. There was no need for sleep and not much for eating. History was being made then and there, and I was a participant.

The FMLN commanders came out to address a roaring crowd and between interruptions from chants and applause, delivered an upbeat and hope-filled pronouncement. Camera flashes lit up the now overflowing lot like daytime. Also among the people were government photographers, who took shot after shot of anyone they could focus on.

Twenty-one days later, the hard right delivered their opinion of the talks. On the morning of the 26th, Herbert Sanabria, president of the Salvadoran Human Rights Commission was assassinated while leaving his home. Hope was nipped in the bud and everyone got back to the business of war.

In 1988, over the objections of traditional hardliners on the right, Roberto D'Abuisson hand-picked Alfredo Cristiani, a relative new comer, to represent the ARENA party in the March 1989 presidential elections. In a relatively easy win over a weakened and corruption-filled PDC, ARENA took power in June of that year.

With the right firmly established in power and the middle ground effectively out of the picture, the stage was set for real negotiations. Almost immediately, Mexican shuttle diplomacy was put into action. A steady deliberate negotiation to end the war began.

The guerrilla offensive of 1989, the smaller push in 1991 and the government strategy to retake well known towns within guerrilla territory without going after the rebels in the surrounding hills, were all maneuvers to achieve better bargaining positions at the negotiation table.

The signing of the peace accords ending the armed conflict in El Salvador took place in Mexico on January 16, 1992. Cristiani became known as *the peace president.* Duarte is known as a well intentioned but powerless leader.

Post War
El Salvador

Guerrilla Construction Inc.

After the peace process was established and the cease fire held, many of the international organizations began packing their bags. The war was over. UN and European Community programs would take over the reconstruction phase. There was no longer the need, nor the resources, for the smaller NGOs that had accompanied communities through the conflict. Downsizing and working through local organizations became the new operating strategy.

To me it felt like cutting and running. Emergency assistance during a conflict is an urgent need and one that is fairly easy to raise money for. The very nature of emergency assistance shrugs off detailed planning and follow-up reporting unlike the procedures necessary for real development. Running out at this critical point in time struck me as irresponsible. We were leaving just as the need for serious long-term work occurred.

I tried to make the case to the Lutheran World Federation for staying and working on pilot development projects. We had been talking about sustainable development for years while the conflict made it impossible. Now, when the conditions would actually allow it, we were backing out. I was told that conditions now allowed the Federation to work through local church structures and that actually the Federation was no longer needed to directly implement projects. I knew that meant an abrupt end to the work I had been doing with communities in the east and it also meant a concentration of resources around San Salvador. I also knew that my service contract with them was about to expire.

At that time a director from Geneva arrived to oversee part of the transition. He heard my argument and was very understanding, but responded, “Well, that’s the way we work throughout the world.” He offered me a post in Angola.

“I’m sure Angola is a lovely place,” I replied, “but I can’t leave here now that the real work is starting.”

He smiled and said, “You’ll be back. Everyone who leaves always comes back.”

Had he known me better, he would have known that there was no better way to make sure I’d never go back. Or perhaps he did and that was the purpose.

“Put your money where your mouth is” has always struck me as a practical part of personal definition. I decided to get out of the NGO world and stay in El Salvador, thereby entering the *real world.*

In post-war El Salvador, a major problem, and at the same time a good opportunity, was the lack of infrastructure. Housing became a major need with the resettlement of conflict areas and the return of former combatants to civilian life. I had been working with re-insertion programs and had construction background, so it seemed natural to set up a construction company incorporating ex-guerrillas as partners and workers. It was a romantic venture, converting guerrillas into construction workers and rebuilding war-torn communities within the country.

Setting up the corporation required a lot of paperwork and legal procedures, but again I jumped in over my head and learned on the job. I figured that if it had been done before, I could do it too. The corporate papers were drawn up with seven partners that were all ex-guerrillas except for me.

Ana Guadalupe was the partner who represented shares set aside for the construction workers. Later this would raise eyebrows when I went to a bank or the credit office of large suppliers because Ana and some of the other partners were well known in their former capacity as guerrilla commanders. Actually, everyone in the firm was an ex-guerrilla, from the office staff to the guys in the field. No one had any investment money, so I put up the required beginning capital.

We started up with two jobs in Segundo Montes, in Morazán. They were a kindergarten center and a health clinic. Our lack of capital and the need to compete in bidding against cutthroat engineers quickly resulted in a financial deficit. We soon found it necessary to take on new jobs just to be able to finish the old ones.

We were training our workers on site. We actually had a blackboard set up and held classes for a couple of hours each morning. We had everyone enrolled in Social Security and were paying by the day as opposed to paying by production.

Some of the guys would just stop working when it got too hot, "Well, you know, we are the owners of the company."

Before long, we had accumulated a sizable deficit and started to look for a bit of help.

We received help for the business from a very unexpected source. Jaime Hill, from one of the wealthy banking families, had been kidnapped and held for ransom by the ERP during the early years of the war. As the peace process developed, Jaime came forward and offered assistance to his former captors during the reinsertion phase. I was honored to be invited to weekly meetings with him where he shared his knowledge of the Salvadoran business and construction world. Jaime Hill assisted us along the way by providing an engineer, an architect and an accountant, who were instrumental in getting us on the right track.

In a two-year period we worked on eight different housing projects totaling some three hundred homes, along with a few clinics and markets. We managed to pull ourselves out of the deficit by the end of the housing phase of the reconstruction.

We made an attempt to enter the commercial housing market by obtaining land with promissory notes. We worked up the plans and permits, but were stonewalled by the financial sector. With no way to break into the tightly guarded circle of banks, construction firms and suppliers, we ended up selling ready-made projects to other firms who had access to the financial system.

With the housing phase of reconstruction in its final days and knowing the difficulty of breaking into the commercial housing market, we decided to cease operation as a construction firm. I bought out the other partners thinking I could use the corporation for some activity in the future and moved back to Morazán. I was getting back to my roots.

The construction phase of the corporation was a great learning experience, but I was glad to be past those sleepless nights when I worried about where I was going to find enough cash for payroll. Getting out without going broke seemed to be a smashing success and I was actually able to double the investment each partner had made.

Today many of the *master builders* or local contractors for building homes in Morazán, are graduates of that romantic beginning of a guerrilla construction firm.

The Sharks of New York

The ending of the war in El Salvador created a tremendous need for reconstruction. It was a big challenge and a great opportunity.

Ana Guadalupe, an ERP commander on the FMLN negotiation team, had made a good connection in New York City. A group of investors wanted to explore the possibility of working with the ERP in the reconstruction process. I was given the job of following up and working out details. The contacts were made and H, a building contractor with the New York group, would be coming down for an assessment.

I picked up H at the airport and we headed off for a tour of the ERP war zones. Our objective was to form a strong development/construction outfit to provide basic housing and livelihood opportunity to the ex-combatants. H seemed to understand what we wanted, asked the right questions and gave good tips. At each site, he would ask how much territory we had and how much labor and then would propose mega projects such as beach resorts or sewing factories for exporters. We were able get him back on track with housing needs and basic services, but were a little concerned about his misconception about land tenure.

It seemed that H had the idea that areas under ERP control during the war were the property of the party and that the ex-combatants were free labor. It was an antique eastern bloc model. We put it down as a lack of knowledge of the situation in El Salvador. He was a little overboard with the consortium controlling everything and he was way out of our comfort zone with some of his ideas, like casinos along the coast for non-existent cruise ships. However, these guys were big league and it was our chance to get a leg up.

Our next meeting was in New York. I flew there with Ana Guadalupe, which felt very strange. After years of clandestine meetings and trying to be careful, there I was, walking through US customs with a well-known FMLN leader. Ana went off to her meetings and I went off with H, to continue our empire building.

H's office was on the third or fourth floor of one of those indistinguishable grey office buildings just a few blocks from the Empire State Building. The next floor up was a modeling agency which made for a great elevator ride. They were all cover girls, tall and slender with giggles and perky nipples staring back at eye level.

H had a standard office with people pushing paper around. I was struck at how modest his office was. It was Spartan. There was not a lot of stuff stacked around, like the mess mine was always in.

Three blocks away was an Irish bar, where lunch went on for hours with too many beers. Another block and a half away was a strip joint. Big city life was a new adventure. There were quick visits to offices to see GPS surveying equipment, design software and garment importers. And a lot of talk. I was educated on roll funds, something about buying currency before it goes into circulation, the Sheik of Dubai, offshore banking, self-leasing and a lot of other ways to work as a consortium.

Rather than leave me all alone in the big city, H would take me to his place, upstate, about an hour and a half away. We would also pick up his girlfriend, a young Korean woman. The house was a two story country home in the suburbs.

Walking in, I was struck at how modest it was, just like the office. It felt like a safe-house. Just the right furniture, everything was new, no odors and no lived-in feeling.

"Just moved in and haven't unpacked yet," said H, catching my look and then pointed out a clay crock out back where his girlfriend was fermenting cabbage for some Korean dish.

"Sure," I replied, "It takes a while to settle into a new place," while thinking, "Yea, right."

I had been in safe-houses before. I had even set up a few when the negotiation process required the guerrilla diplomatic corps to come down out of the hills. This sure felt like one. I began to have my doubts about H.

A couple of days into the visit, I took some time to go to a book store. My favorite author at the time was Graham Greene and every time I went stateside I would search out one of his books. This time, I also picked up Sun Tzu's "The Art of War" and another book in the same section on how to persuade people to do what you want. It explained CIA methods and procedures.

The next day we went back to H's office. After nearly having my eye gouged out in the elevator by a particularly bouncy model, we settled down to coffee and planning the day's activities. Suddenly I noticed something that really surprised me.

H was mimicking every move I made. If I sat back, he would sit back. When I crossed my legs, so did he. If I put my elbow on the table, he followed suit. It was unbelievable.

The chapter in the new book I had read the night before described the technique that H was using on me. Basically, the technique is to mimic your target until you reach their comfort zone. Then you start making the new moves. If your target follows your moves, he is open and ready for your suggestions. I tried a couple of moves just to be sure and H followed right along.

H is a spook, I thought. What have I gotten myself into?

I think H realized then that I was becoming a bit wary. However, our time together was almost over, with the only remaining major activity being a meeting with L, the head of the investor group.

L's office was the real thing. A working office cluttered with stacks of paper, photos on the wall and personal trinkets lying around. It was small, but a power office, smelling of Cuban cigars, on the second floor with a big window behind him overlooking Times Square.

Ana Guadalupe had not yet arrived, so L lit up a Cuban and offered the box to me. We began with small talk until Ana arrived.

The proposal was straight forward. The investor group wanted representation rights for the reconstruction and development of the ERP areas of influence. All projects and programs would be managed from the New York office and of course we would get a piece of the action. Everything started to click in my head. Everything H had been feeding me was designed to lure us into the underworld of high finance.

Ana didn't need all the background information; she had more than enough experience to know where this was leading.

When L turned his back to us to look through his window, she cut off my translation. "I get the gist," she said, rolling her eyes, "Now, why don't you tell him our proposal."

Caught off guard, I winged it. I understood she did not want to address the proposal directly, nor say anything that could be interpreted as an agreement. It was going to be up to me to deal with the situation, make a counter offer and end the meeting inconclusively.

"That's a very interesting proposal," I said, "We like what we see here, and actually, what we had in mind was to invite you to join in the formation of a Salvadoran construction firm. For five hundred thousand, we would be willing to let you have forty-nine percent."

The counter offer had the desired effect and the meeting ended with the agreement to consider each other's offer.

"You have a nice town here, L" and "Have a good trip back," were the parting phrases.

Several months later, H made a follow-up visit to El Salvador. He arrived a little less energetic, more wary, and seemed to have been sent to salvage something from the time and effort invested. He left with what seemed to be his forgone conclusion; no progress on representation or the consortium.

Later, during the process of privatization of public utilities in El Salvador, I received a series of phone calls from H, asking about procedures for privatization. I again grew wary when he asked about Joaquin Villalobos' contacts and friendships with people in the privatization process, or in the utility companies themselves. Joaquin was the head commander of the ERP and had well known contacts and friendships with high officials. One in particular was with the head of the telephone company.

When H asked if I thought it would be possible to get an inside line on the telephone company through Joaquin, our relationship hit a wall.

Later, I mentioned the situation to Joaquin and he said, "We didn't spend twenty years fighting in the hills, to walk down and take a part in corruption. If that's what they're looking for, cut them off."

Receiving yet another half expected answer, H stopped all communication and we never got our taste of the underworld of high finance.

The Other Side of the Barrier

I needed to have Ana Guadalupe sign some business papers for the construction firm. She was too busy to come to my office and asked me to come to hers. She had been elected to Congress so her office was on the eighth floor of the National Assembly Building.

I drove down early that morning, fighting the crazy rush hour traffic and basically driving in circles until I found a parking space. Since the ending of the war there had been a tremendous increase in the numbers of vehicles on the road, with over three thousand used cars and trucks imported per month. Even one of the courts where we used to play basketball with the journalists during the war years had been converted to a parking lot for the Assembly Building. I had to use the dusty lot on the other side of the street.

Security around the Assembly Building was tight. First I went through a police checkpoint, marked off with barbed wire at the perimeter of the building. There I was checked for weapons and asked what my business was. Next I had to go through internal security at the door, with the same procedure and questions. Finally I got to the reception desk where it was necessary to trade my identification card for a clip-on card identifying the floor I was allowed to visit.

When I finally reached Ana's office, I had to wait for her to finish a meeting, so I was offered a cup of coffee. Office coffee is typically a weak tea like brew that comes already sugared, but it's better than nothing and gave me something to do. After seeing the aftermath of the 86 earthquake, I didn't like spending much time in buildings like this where you could see the patched-up cracks running up through the walls. So, I took the coffee.

Our appointment had been set for nine o'clock. Even after fifteen years of living in El Salvador I was still in the habit of showing up on time for appointments. While growing up, my father always had the clock set fifteen minutes early, so that even if we left late we could make it to church on time. Church was a fifteen minute drive away. People generally confuse the Latin American habit of showing up *late* as a sign of discourtesy or laziness. Actually they are normally punctual, within their concept of time management. For them, nine o'clock is the period of time between nine and ten o'clock. Before laughing that off as preposterous, consider what *we* do with ages. When asked our age, we state our age at our last birthday, even if we are a week away from our next one.

Ana came breezing in, punctually, about forty-five minutes later, and signed the papers. As we were doing the usual small talk, word came that the building had been taken over by a group of demonstrators. As we looked down from the window, a mob formed around the building. We could see several guys unloading bulky backpacks in the bushes, so we knew it was a serious situation. I can't recall exactly who they were, but I think they were from the ex-civil defense groups who had not benefited from the post-war programs. I accepted more coffee.

It was an interesting experience. I had been in this type of situation before, but on the other side of the barrier. When Herbert Sanabria, the president of the Salvadoran Human Rights Commission was assassinated in 1987, I went with the traveling wake. With a hat pulled down over my eyes and wearing a loose jacket, I spent a couple of nights with Herbert's body and the big crowd at the doors of the US embassy. I had often accompanied local organizations for this type of event, not as an active participate, but just as an accompanying presence. Besides, some of these groups had some very attractive women. A chilly night with a touch of danger and a growing group spirit for a common cause oddly enough can create a very romantic setting.

This new situation of being on the inside was anything but romantic. Several members of Congress were ex-military, some with the guerrilla and other with the government forces. They started making plans on barricades and evacuation, and even talked of bringing in helicopters to take us off the roof. Mostly though, we just sat and drank coffee, office coffee. Not everyone was adventurous enough to consider making a break for it. Nothing much happened all day, except that the electricity was cut off.

I was told that I should probably report to the U.S. Embassy, so I called in. No one was there, of course, and I could hear the call re-routing. It was probably answered by someone up in Virginia.

"No, I don't think I am in danger, just informing you of the situation. Don't send in the Seals just yet."

The Civilian Police Force finally made its way in around eight o'clock that night and announced that they were negotiating to get us safe passage. The police commissioner in charge of our safety was an extremely nervous young woman who kept pulling out her gun to see if the safety was on. She alternated between telling us to get ready to go and to sit and wait awhile. Sometimes it looked like she was building up the nerve to shoot her way out of the situation. Ready to go out in a blaze of glory, she was.

Finally, after several hours, our release was negotiated. We got in line to file down the eight flights of stairs. The stairwell was dark and the only flashlight around was the one carried by the nervous policewomen at the front of the line. So we slowly groped our way down, one hand on the railing and the other on the back of the person in front of us.

When we arrived at the lobby and started pushing through the demonstrators to reach the exit, I was flagged down by the guy at the receptionist desk. I guess he hadn't moved the whole time.

"You've got to sign out," he said, holding out my identification card, "Let me have your pass. Thank you, you can go now," as he neatly tucked the pass back into its numbered slot.

He appeared to be totally oblivious to the events going on around him.

Tale of Two Mayors

J is the outgoing mayor of a small mountain town in Morazán. He belongs to the right-wing ARENA party. J is conservative, nationalistic and basically follows the party line promoting personal liberty, private enterprise and the other standard right-wing banners.

M is the incoming mayor and she belongs to the revolutionary FMLN party. She follows the liberal party line of generally socialist alignment. This is M's third period as mayor. She was voted into office during the elections that followed the peace accords and held the office for two terms. After the one term of an ARENA mayor, she returned for another two terms and then lost the office to J.

Both J and M fit nicely into their roles as leaders of the right and left, respectively. One would be inclined to believe that both of them have a history that fits as nicely into those left/right divisions. After all, is not the FMLN a party of former guerrillas and ARENA the party of former governmental supporters?

Well, let's spiral back in time to 1984, back to the heavy *real fighting* of the civil war, before it went *low intensity.* Where were J and M then? The civil war in El Salvador, for all intents and purposes, was one of the more straightforward components of the east-west conflict, was it not? It was a fairly black and white situation, depending of the political stance of the observer. We would naturally place J with the governmental forces, either as military or at least a supporter. M, more than likely would be one of the thousands of brave female FMLN combatants or someone in the support structure.

Actually, I first met M on a spring morning in 1984 in the Buenos Aires refugee camp in Honduras. It was near the small Honduran town of Colomoncagua, just across the border from the Morazán war zone in El

Salvador. The town was host to two refugee camps: the large Colomoncagua camp filled with some eight thousand Salvadorans considered to be leftists and guerrilla supporters, and the Buenos Aires camp of a few dozen rightists considered to be government supporters. I was in the camp that morning with the UNHCR representative. We were assessing the housing needs of the refugees when M and her husband O came walking across the field carrying their one-year old son and a bag of belongings.

O had been forcibly recruited by the ERP, the FMLN force active in Morazán. After several weeks of training, O was given the choice of staying with the guerrillas or leaving the area. He and M left, seeking refuge in Honduras.

During this same time period, J, far from supporting the government, was risking life and limb as a logistics supplier for the ERP. Logistics meant living a dangerous double life, posing as a civilian while supplying the guerrillas with food, boots, batteries and anything else an army needs to operate. Any slip up by J would have been met with instant and probably painful death.

Another black and white situation, only the roles have changed. When our political views are fixed and we have divided the participants into heroes and villains, how do we reconcile this seeming complete switching of roles?

Looking Back

Origin of the War

I have never heard a complete explanation of the origin of the Civil War in El Salvador. The standard story of fourteen families owning the country, while true, is superficial and falls short of the complex realities that were at play. While I am no academic nor do I claim to be an expert on the subject, the bits and pieces of information, news, hearsay and empirical analysis have led me to form my own opinion.

The Salvadoran situation should be looked at on four different levels: national, regional, international and world. Of course there are factors that overlap from one level to another and some of the pieces do not fit without some acceptance of *behind the scene* players and interests seemingly at odds with the interested parties own policy.

On the national level, El Salvador was a feudal state up through the seventies. With a land-based economic structure, the political and economic power was completely controlled by the large land owners, the infamous fourteen families. This was the group of *old money* and numbered approximately two hundred strong, the descendants of the original Spanish land holders. Their power was reinforced by military dictatorships and the military forces that were at their beck and call. Indeed, they installed and disposed of the dictators at their whim. Among the disenfranchised under this system were the landless peasants, the incipient middle class professionals, commerce and the *new money* industrialists.

On the regional level, all of Latin America was in turmoil, as it had been for the past eighty years. The ongoing US policy was, as expressed so eloquently by Franklin D. Roosevelt during the Somoza dynasty in Nicaragua, "He's a son of a bitch, but he's our son of a bitch." This clashed with the spirit of John Kennedy's Alliance for Progress. On the one hand, creating hope and, on the other, crushing it.

Look no further than the history of the US banana industry in Latin America to see the paradox of lip service to political freedoms and covert military operations for the benefit of US corporations with a vested interest in maintaining the feudal system. The Sandinista victory in Nicaragua in 1979 was a flash point that led to an escalation of interest and intervention on the international level.

On the international level, the mutually beneficial *Cold War* between the Soviet Union and the US was carried out by proxy throughout Africa, Asia and Latin America. Preventing the raging fire of communist revolution that threatened to sweep through Latin America and straight into Texas was the battle cry of successive US administrations. The Soviet Bloc and its allies, including Cuba, provided arms, training and some finances to insurgency groups throughout the region. Contrary to popular belief however, Moscow and Havana did not see eye to eye on strategy and purpose and did not present a united front of support, in the case of El Salvador.

On the world level, Toffler's theory of the rise and fall of civilizations comes into play. By the late seventies, the *civilized world* was well on into the Industrial Age, and showing signs of moving into the Information Age. Latin America in general and El Salvador in particular, was frozen in time in the Agricultural Age, operating under a feudal system. Considering the current state of the Industrial Age, along with changing world wide political and economic structure would put El Salvador some two hundred years behind time. Evolution denied sparks revolution.

Now, take the dynamics from each level and concentrate them in an area of 8,124 square miles with a population of four million people. Add to the mix the influx of European and Palestinian immigrants in the period of 1920 through the late forties and the influence of Liberation Theology.

The two World Wars resulted in a continuous flow of European and Middle Eastern immigrants searching for new opportunities. Many of them came to Latin America. The subsequent creation of the state of Israel caused another massive migration from the Middle East, much of which came to Central America.

The European migration came in the form of adventure seekers, primarily from England and Germany, who got off the boat with a backpack and promptly married the richest available girl in town. They became the *new money* group of fledging industrialists.

The Palestinians, primarily Christians from Bethlehem, came as families and settled into trade, commerce, textiles and banking.

The representation of these immigrants is significant and any name search of business leaders in El Salvador will turn up many European and Palestinian surnames. Indeed the Palestinian population in the country today is close to one hundred thousand.

These groups had no political participation under the feudal system, and that could only be gained by bringing down the established power structure within the country. They aligned themselves on both sides of the conflict. Recognizing the need to break the hold of the feudal system, a significant amount of covert financial aid to the revolutionary forces did come from these sectors, even some of those considered to be *unaligned.*

The apparent change in doctrine reflected in the Second Vatican Council, together with growing concern among clergy regarding the social injustice directed primarily against the poor in Latin America, led to a series of liberationist theories and writings regarding the church's *preferential option for the poor.*

Liberation Theology was born and it spread like wildfire through the poor communities in Latin America, largely through the Jesuit order. It stressed the need for political activism as a means of achieving social justice and eliminating poverty. Liberation Theology does not shy away from fingering exploitive capitalism as the root source of poverty and as a sin against God and Mankind. Group discussions led to the forming of Christian-Based Communities, which eventually motivated part of the participants to join the armed struggle.

The irony is that when El Salvador came out of the war, the world had changed completely. Access to land served only for subsistence, no longer as a power base. The Industrial Age had come and gone, replaced by the Information Age with its strong financial component. The Berlin Wall had been pulled down and Russia and the US were getting rather friendly. Other than that media show of a war by the Zapatistas in Mexico, the era of open conflict had ended in Latin America. The immediate privatization of public utilities, pension funds and banks, after the war, transferred the center of power to faceless international corporations. Even the church was pulling back from its *preferential option for the poor.* With the exception of the need for genuine political participation, the premises originating the war had largely disappeared.

Common Sense and Lady Luck

Living in a country at war is surprisingly uneventful for the most part. Routines are established, people go to work, children off to school, bills to pay, lines to stand in at the bank, groceries to buy and all the boring day to day activities, just like anywhere else in the world. Basketball in the afternoon twice a week with the journalists, Saturday night parties, Sunday down at the beach with friends, rounding out the normal urban activities.

Suddenly out of nowhere, everything changes; gunshots ring out or a bomb goes off, and everyone scurries for cover. Five minutes later, as the dust settles, a few people tentatively step out to see if the danger has passed. Before you know it, everything is back to normal, back to the routine.

Getting around safely requires a combination of common sense, gut feelings and the kind blessings of Lady Luck. Common sense is fairly straight forward. Try to fit in and don't stand out too much. Never look lost, always go as with a purpose. If it doesn't look right, turn around right away. And never ever loiter close to a military target. Gut feelings are just that, no rationale, but never argue with them. God, Lady Luck and your Guardian Angels are extremely generous. Just be thankful.

Back in 88, I was taking a couple of Brits out to San Miguel for a meeting with a *campesino* (farmers) cooperative organization. It was their first day in the country and they were eager to see the sites and get to know the situation in the east.

We got a late start to the day and I was trying to make up for lost time on the Pan-American Highway. As we got into the series of sharp curves leading into the Lempa River basin, I almost back ended a slow moving military truck with a couple of soldiers sitting on top of the load of supplies. I swerved around them.

"Funny to see a military truck out here all by itself," I commented to the newcomers, "Normally they travel in convoys."

Around the next curve, we came upon another truck, this one packed with men in civilian clothing.

"New recruits," I explained, "Each Colonel goes out and rounds up a new batch when his troop level gets too low."

"This is the wrong place to be," I muttered as each curve revealed another truck to be passed.

"Actually, this is something you never want to do," I informed my passengers, "but we are running late for the meeting. I think we are almost through, only two more trucks ahead."

As I pulled over into the passing lane to get by a truckload of soldiers, something stopped me. I began braking to fall back behind. We were some three car lengths behind, when suddenly the soldiers standing on the left side of the truck lifted into the air, floating like thrown rag dolls against the slats on the other side.

The blast of the claymore brought me to my senses while watching the surreal scene in front of us and I swerved off the road into a shallow ditch, parking up against one of those giant Ceiba trees. I shoved the Brits out of the passenger side and got them behind the wheels of the Jeep. The ensuing five minute fire-fight was all one-sided as the soldiers emptied out clip after clip on the surrounding hills. No shots were fired back.

As the shooting died down, a middle-aged woman wearing a white apron came out of the brush behind, smiling down at us in the ditch while casually brushing off her hands.

On one of my trips into the war zone of Morazán, I was asked to take along a passenger. I was not told who she was and did have my suspicions, but agreed to give her a ride. The day we were to leave San Salvador, my red Jeep broke down and had to be put in the shop. I was able to borrow the Jeep of a friend. It was the same model as mine except for the color, this one was blue.

We spent the night at a cheap hotel in San Miguel, The China House about three blocks away from the Third Brigade. San Miguel is hot, even at night the heat rises off the pavement and ground turning any closed room into a sauna. The air-conditioner in the room at the China House was so loud it was impossible to sleep, and without it much too warm to sleep.

We left around four in the morning to head north. As we came out of the parking lot, I turned right, on a whim. My normal route would have been to the left, up through Ciudad Barrios and across at Carolina. It was the route I had planned to take and in fact my passenger was to be met at that entry point. It just didn't feel right, so I went the other way.

As we approached Osicala, my passenger suddenly sat up and asked where we were.

"Oh my God," she exclaimed when I told her, "This is my home town, everyone here knows me."

"Fine time to be telling me," I muttered as we were stopped at a checkpoint that shouldn't have been there.

Normally the military checkpoints were up and running at six in the morning. It was five twenty and dawn was just about to break. These guys must have a new officer or be on some special mission. Told we could not pass and would have to go back to Gotera to get special permission, I asked to see the commanding officer. I was directed into the town to the garrison. I told my passenger to keep her cool, keep her sunglasses and hat on and to pretend to be sleeping. It took some twenty minutes, but I was finally able convince the commander to allow us to pass.

We got out just as the townsfolk were starting their daily activity and my passenger breathed a big sigh of relief as we left the bumpy cobble stoned streets behind. When we arrived at the *Witches Pool* on the Torola River, she told me she couldn't swim and wanted to find another way across.

I put my foot down when she asked some local boys "if any enemy was around" and convinced her to strip down and get pulled across like everyone else. I did though take the time to tie a decent knot that she couldn't slip out of.

Later that afternoon, my passenger safely delivered, I began the journey back to San Salvador. No sooner than I had left the community of San Isidro, down by the river, an approaching car flagged me down.

"Be careful up ahead," warned a lady I took to be a health care worker. "I don't know if it has anything to do with you," she said in hushed tones so that her driver couldn't overhear, "but there are road blocks all over looking for a gringo in a red Jeep carrying someone very important."

She went on to explain that from what she was told, the red jeep was expected over towards Carolina and when it didn't come through during the early morning, the search was widened to the whole northern zone.

I thanked her, "Couldn't be me, but thanks for the warning."

Somewhere between San Simon and Osicala I turned uphill into the labyrinth of dirt roads crisscrossing the coffee plantations of Cacauatíque. I felt my way through to the outskirts of Ciudad Barrios, just as dusk was falling. Needless to say, I never used the red Jeep again in the east. I believe we donated it to a local organization in Chalatenango.

On another occasion, up in guerrilla territory around Torola, I was requested to meet one of the commanders in Perquín. The walk from Torola to Perquín was always a pleasant stroll, a nice wide road shaded by towering trees on both sides, leaf covered and smooth, and most importantly, it was on the level. After the three hour hike straight up from the river to Torola, walking on the level makes one feel buoyant and leaves a spring to the step. The cool afternoon breeze, birds singing in chorus and the sun-dappled path ahead always brought to mind hiking on the Appalachian Trail, leaving the war far behind.

So I headed off to Perquín that afternoon with Moncho as my guide. *Moncho, who was often my guide back behind the lines, is a tall lanky guy, friendliest character you could ever run across, but just a tad out of sync with the rest of the world. A real Forrest Gump type. How he survived the war is a mystery to me, but he is still around. Sometimes he works the newspaper route, sometimes picks up odds jobs.*

Anyway, we were strolling along the trail, Moncho sauntering along with his AKA slung over his back, paying more attention to his transistor radio than anything else and me just enjoying the feeling of stretching out my leg tendons on a level walk.

Suddenly, the hair on the back of my neck stood up and I knew we were being watched. I could see no one around and nothing happened, but I could not shake the feeling until we had advanced a half mile or so.

Years later, an Irish volunteer would tell me a story about a man in one of the communities where she worked. It seems the man had asked her if she knew me. When she said yes, he proceeded to relate the story of how he met me. He had been in the army, in a special operations group called the PRAL. The PRAL were units of four to five specialized members who would insert themselves deep within guerrilla territory and lie in wait for days on end, to ambush important targets. This man told the Irish volunteer that he had me in his sights and was ready to shoot, but decided against it at the last minute as he didn't know exactly who I was. No way, of course, of comparing notes to corroborate the date and time, but for me there is not a shred of doubt of where and when that took place.

Common sense is a basic tool for staying alive. Paying attention to gut feelings will get you further, but when the situation is out of your hands the generosity of Lady Luck is essential.

Sympathy and Alignment

Close enough to get singed, but not burned. That is the fine line you walk while working with a civilian population in the midst of a civil war. The human suffering faced by communities that find themselves in conflict zones and those considered to be aligned with the insurgency will create a deep feeling of sympathy within anyone assisting them.

The very nature of civil war and the strategic implementation of guerrilla warfare create varying degrees of alignment within the civilian population.

This ranges from sympathy to outright participation with the insurgency. Civil rights abuses against aligned communities seem to be tacitly accepted by the international powers that be. The blanket argument of neutrality is used by communities as a defensive protective measure.

An inexperienced international aid worker quickly becomes sympathetic with the suffering *neutral population.* However, as the level of confidence grows between the aid worker and individuals in the community, the layers of neutrality begin to peel back. At this point one of two reactions will occur; the aid worker will pull back to the safety of previous concepts or will start a gradual process of transference of sympathy to the aligned elements in the community.

It is amusing to recall the many debates and arguments between the international workers, as this transference of sympathy would lead to defense of the political and military strategies of one or another group within the FMLN. While I did some work with communities under the control of each of the five factions of the guerrilla forces, most of my effort was in the ERP controlled areas of Usulután, San Miguel and Morazán. Therefore, I had a natural tendency to cheer lead their direct manner of carrying out the war as opposed to the sluggish *prolonged people's struggle* of the FPL in Chalatenango.

Where exactly is the line drawn between sympathy and alignment? The development of relationships with individuals and families within the communities converts that question from a purely academic or moral realm into a personal issue. *These are my friends being abused* and *Of course they have the right to fight back* can very quickly turn to *How can I help them?* Personal high moral positions such as non-violence, whether by conviction or upbringing, are seriously questioned, generating an internal battle between mind and gut.

Institutional responsibility is quickly viewed and then tossed out as irrelevant.

Fear is a major factor. Fear of what happens if you get caught and fear of the misunderstanding *back home* when you are labeled, fear of no safe return route.

Citizenship, never even thought of before, suddenly becomes relevant. My country is supporting the wrong side for the wrong reasons. Even while paying lip service to human rights and congressional hearings, rogue administrations run covert operations and turn a blind eye to their crony's actions. Many times the thought process will be, "I am just a much a citizen as that ass running things and I am here on the ground where those policies play out."

There are no guide posts out there marking the limits and personal restraints get shredded. In the end, there are no big decisions made, just small, day-to-day efforts to maintain a balance.

While on a family visit to Delaware, years after the war had ended, I noticed a newspaper clipping my mother had put in the photo album. It was a photo of two wounded guerrillas sitting against the wall in a bombed out house. When I asked, my mother admitted that she and my dad were sure that one of the guys in the photo was me.

Clearly, I wasn't the only one who had gone through the anguish of which route I was to take.

Non-Violence

"Let me see that," said G one day, as he slipped the pistol from my waistband, "that's a pretty little gun you got there."

He looked me straight in the eyes, "You've never had to kill anyone, have you?"

Not even waiting for an answer, he continued, "You know if someone has had to kill by the gun they carry...."

His eyes dulled over and his voice went into deadpan mode, "You have no idea how hard it is to kill a man.

You find out when you have to execute someone standing right in front of you. You just want to get it over with."

After a pause, he continued, "The first time I was sent to execute a man, there were three of us, I had a 9mm and the other guys had peashooters as well... the guy wouldn't die, he kept getting up and coming at us. It must have taken twelve shots to keep him down and he was still breathing. From that day on I never carry anything less than a 45."

He handed the pistol back. "That's a pretty little gun you got there," he repeated.

I never carried a gun during the war. The day the war ended, I borrowed a Colt 45 and a few weeks later I bought a 9mm. Carrying a gun in my work during the war was impossible. That would have meant going over, crossing the line, becoming an organic member of the insurgency. Starting a relationship with Marisol, an ERP commander, practically on the eve of the signing of the peace accords, made the weapon a practical necessity. While the end of the war was a joyous and momentous event, there was still an air of uncertainty because not everyone was satisfied with the outcome. Death threats and hostile posturing were the order of the day and it seemed somewhat irresponsible not to have a means of defense.

Once again, stepping fully out of my element, I accompanied Marisol to the ceremonies and public events marking the end of the war. As a VIP in the demobilizing guerrilla force, Marisol had two full time bodyguards assigned to her, but I just couldn't leave everything in their hands.

The day after I bought the 9mm, I headed back to Morazán looking for Mario. Mario is a Nicaraguan who had been through the Sandinista Revolution and then came to El Salvador during the early days of the conflict as a weapons instructor.

"If I'm going to be carrying this thing around, I want to know how to use it," I told Mario.

We walked over a couple of hills to an unpopulated area away from the road for my crash course.

Mario gave some practical advice before starting, "You'll never get into a long distance fire fight, anything longer than from one side of the street to the other is a waste of time, don't even think about it."

As he paced off some twenty strides and hung a paper plate target on a scrubby pine, I protested that it was too close.

"This is as far away as it gets," he cut me off, "and remember, the target is shooting back."

Mario let me shoot two rounds to get the feel of the new pistol before stopping me for the real lesson.

"Put your gun back where you carry it and as you carry it. How do you carry it? A round in the chamber? Cocked or uncocked? Safety on or off?" he fired off the questions.

"Look," he said, "the street is not a firing range where you have time to set up. Always carry your weapon the same, and decide right now how that is going to be."

He went on, "You're on the defense. That means the other guy gets a shot off first. If he is nervous or inexperienced, the shot will go high, so you crouch as you pull. Let two shots off, aim low on the first one, the recoil will elevate the second one and then crouch more to your right for one more shot. That's as long as it goes, by now one of you are down."

A couple of hours and a box and a half of shells later, I was declared a *killer shot.*

The graphic depiction from G and the shooting lessons with Mario had a sobering effect on me. Even with the experience of living in a country at war and being under fire, I had never contemplated the mechanics involved in killing someone face to face. The internal debate I had gone through before, regarding non-violence, now seemed like a purely academic exercise. Now I had the means in my hands. Now real decisions would have to be made and made in a split second.

The romantic tie with Marisol meant a social association with the inner circle of the ERP leadership. On the New Years Eve following the peace accords, we were at a party in Joaquin Villalobos' house when Joaquin decided he wanted to go downtown to buy fireworks. Joaquin was the top ERP commander and one of the signatories of the Peace Accords. The peace process was going well, but had not been completed, so security was still a big issue.

When he realized that he had only one bodyguard present at the time with a permit to carry a weapon, he turned to me.

"You got a permit for that gun?"

"Sure," I stuttered, "I've got a permit."

"Great, let's go," he said, and off we went for another surreal experience.

"How in the world did you get yourself into this?" I grumbled under my breath while trying to look grim and tough for the onlookers while Joaquin bounded gleefully around the outdoor plaza buying up a bunch of fireworks.

The closest I came to using a weapon was when Carmelo, an ERP commander and a very close friend, was assassinated. It was one of those situations that was never cleared up. On the eve of his assassination, death threats started again, very explicit and personally directed at the leadership of the ERP. Marisol, Luisa and I holed up in one the offices for the night, expecting the worst. For this occasion I was given an AKA. It was actually on the waiting list to be turned over to the UN, but had not yet been replaced by a legal weapon. The phone calls continued all night and cars were constantly circling, but nothing happened.

I was raised as a pacifist in the Mennonite Church. Throughout my time in Honduras and El Salvador, I struggled with the concept. Was it personal conviction or just part of the baggage? Sometimes I think our problem is the need to define something as forever and ever more. I no longer struggle with the issue. I do think that Love is the answer, but I also now trust myself to make the right decision at the right time.

Some Wounds just will not Heal

Marta lost her daughter, two month old Gloria Noemi, during the August 29, 1985, Honduran military attack on the Colomoncagua refugee camp. The baby was snatched from her arms and slaughtered. Sorry, no other description quite fits. Twenty-three years have now gone by. Marta is okay, sometimes. Other times, she walks the roads in Morazán, venting her rage on the hillsides and the clouds in the sky, and on the rest of us. Some people laugh. Some remember her loss that day.

The walking wounded are an embarrassing lot, aren't they? They can't get over it, can't get on with it and can't get with the program. The rest of us focus on economic development, training, services and reconstruction. Politely ignoring those who have wounds that just will not heal.

I have no answers here, just a sincere acknowledgement.

Johnny

Hey Johnny, where 'you walkin?
Way too white to be on that side
Had'u fought for us like you fought for them
Hada bunch of medals pinned to your hide

The case of John Walker, better known as the *American Taliban* gave me pause. Gave me pause and made me mad.

We idolize as heroes those who in the past put conviction before self, who faced death with courage, and who survived insurmountable odds. There seems to be so few around today that there is a need to invent them.

You do not have to share Walker's political views to admit that the guy has spunk. He fought on the front lines and survived a *take no prisoner* policy. He survived that scam at the prison which, by design or not, eliminated many of his fellow prisoners. He then spent days holing up in a flooded basement, with water and sewage up to his nose.

What if he had done that for the *other side* or had done it while the Taliban were still allies? He would have so much brass hanging off his chest that it would be impossible for him to stand straight up.

I do not condone John Walker's actions, neither do I condemn them. I do though, admire the guy and respect his courage.

Completely different circumstances and paths cannot be compared. I do wonder though how close, just how close I could have come.

There is a very fine line visible while running along the edge and sometimes it blurs and almost fades away. So easy to cross over, no restraints, no dilemma, just that soft voice suggesting, "Not yet, perhaps not yet."

Present Day

Perkin Lenca

As housing construction work declined, I began to look for ways to pick up and move to Morazán. I still had about four acres of land on the outskirts of Perquín that I had purchased some years before as a way of moving along a housing project. The organization financing the project did not have enough cash to buy the entire parcel and the owner would not agree to a partial sale. To make the deal work I bought half of the parcel without having any particular idea what I was going to do with it.

Looking at the options for staying in Morazán, the only viable one seemed to be to develop something to do with tourism. All of the economic studies done on the area agreed that tourism was the most economically viable activity for Morazán. So, I decided to build a hotel.

I looked at the hotel as more than a business investment. I wanted a self-sustainable development project that could help create and promote economic growth in one of the poorest areas of the country. I soon found out that no one else viewed it as a good investment.

When I would visit banks, first of all I had to explain where Perquín was located and then face a bewildered, "Why are you doing that there?" and "Hmm, we'll get back to you."

I did proposals, feasibility studies, ten-year projections and even went to Costa Rica to present it to an organization specializing in financing eco-tourism. I met the same response everywhere. Even the local folks weren't sure that enough visitors would actually show up. Finally, I threw out all of the papers and studies before they could convince me to change my mind. I started building the hotel.

The one positive response I got was from a long-time friend, Don Warnick, who encouraged me to move forward and assured me that he would help when possible. My brother Paul, a dairy farmer from Virginia, as well as my other brothers and my mother came through with a lot of support. The building process took two and a half years, partly because of financial constraints and partly because I trained and worked alongside a small group of local guys with a building method unknown in the area.

I must admit that I was so focused on finishing the building the hotel that I completely overlooked the aspect of running it. Somehow I had the idea that building was the difficult part and that once finished I could put people in to run it while I jaunted off around the countryside. That illusion came to an end real quick and I was forced to choose between becoming a failed business owner or a full-time hotelier.

It was gratifying to be able to hire employees whom I had either known from refugee camp days or who had grown up there. It created a re-connect and brought everything back together. While satisfying, it did pose a whole new series of challenges for me. None of my new employees had been formally employed before and none had ever set foot in a hotel or restaurant, other than a fast-food chicken place in Gotera. Water closets or toilets were a first for several, so that's where the training began. It was a learning experience for all of us, especially for me as I learned the ropes on the job.

Thirteen years have now gone by and the hotel has turned out to be that self-sustaining project. It is currently maintaining some twenty-five, local, full-time employees and giving a push to the tourism industry for the area.

It hasn't been a big money maker yet, but allows a steady growth and a decent livelihood. In comparison to industry norms, I probably tend to keep too many employees around and may go a little overboard with benefits and with my taxes, but that's part of my nature and background. I didn't come to this point to set aside my ideals and focus wholly on capital gain.

The intangibles remain much more gratifying. I do plan to pay back everyone, one of these days, and I am grateful for their patience. It's just that new opportunities and endeavors keep presenting themselves.

I do believe that we artificially separate our money-making from our humanitarian activities. We often focus on pure capital gain first and view humanitarian activities as a gift which will be diluted away in the sea of never-ending poverty. We demand total efficiency with one and accept much less with the other.

I would challenge that concept and propose a merging of the activities, allowing both to be done efficiently. Otherwise, we maintain a vicious cycle of creating poverty in the name of business efficiency and then dealing with the created problem in a haphazard manner.

I would also challenge any humanitarian program to start out with the hotel's initial investment and have the same long-term sustainable economic and social impact in the community.

Cycles of Poverty

Twenty years have passed since the signing of the peace accords that ended the twelve years of armed conflict in El Salvador. However, for many Salvadorans the ongoing peace process ended on March 15, 2009, with the election of the FMLN candidate as President of El Salvador. The acceptance of the FMLN victory by the right-wing ARENA party marked the end of unilateral dominance in Salvadoran politics.

El Salvador faces many challenges and the well used term *making up for the lost decade* is a very small part of that. In practical terms, one hundred years of stalled social and economic evolution need to be made up for. With a population of some 845 inhabitants per square mile, the return to a land-based economy is out of the question. Heavy industry was not developed during the golden age as it had in many parts of the world. That leaves the economy dependent on two fragile activities, the service industry and the exportation of illegal labor.

The service industry itself is largely aimed at internal consumption, which in turn makes it dependent on the inflow of fresh monies generated by Salvadorans working elsewhere. And they are working illegally for the most part. Economists have estimated that without those remittances from the exterior, the economy of El Salvador would be on par with Haiti. An economic platform built on the back of illegal immigrants is shaky at best and completely unsustainable. The average three hundred Salvadorans deported per week adds to the growing social problem of a post-war generation that has no perspective of a decent future.

The growing concern by US citizens regarding illegal immigrants is understandable, especially with the attention given lately to the *Mara Salvatrucha* and other violent gang organizations.

The immigration story has another side however, which needs to be recognized in order to have the complete picture.

Every day, in the small towns and communities scattered throughout the countryside, dozens upon dozens of families bid farewell to a loved one who has built up enough nerve and funding to set out on the journey north. For the past several weeks, they have not been allowed to do strenuous work and they have been fed and pampered more than ever before. They need to build up their strength for the dangerous days ahead.

The family has hocked everything they own to pay for the trip. Costs will range from a couple thousand dollars for the cheap risky version up to ten thousand for a quick and secure delivery. Children are hugged and told to pay attention to Mommy or Grandma. Spouses get their goodbye kiss and the older folks get a special hug because they probably will not be seen again. Candles are lit to a variety of virgins and saints, and prayers are elevated for a safe journey and the hope that the one going north does not fall into the clutches of drugs and gangs.

Drugs and gangs are the worst nightmare for anyone watching a loved one leave because so many normal young people come back practically unrecognizable. The families depend on their average two hundred dollar remittance once or twice a month. In fact, over sixty percent of bank customers are women and older men. They stand patiently in line with their remittance code, written on tiny pieces of scrap paper, clutched tightly in their hands.

The physical reconstruction of infrastructure in El Salvador has been a long, costly endeavor. Basic public services have never caught up and now must also deal with a rapid population growth.

With over half of the population underage, the public school system struggles at a sub-standard level, dealing with quantity rather than quality. The national budget for public services relies heavily on international loans because internal revenue generation is limited to a very narrow tax base of income tax and added value taxes. These taxes generate very little revenue due to the general state of the economy, as well as a fairly high rate of evasion.

Other major income generating activities are no longer available as revenue sources. Public utilities have all been sold to international corporations, as well as banks, pension funds and even the issuing of national identity cards, drivers licenses and vehicle registration.

The cycles of poverty existing prior to the conflict have largely remained intact, with the exception of the lack of political participation and human rights abuses. Others have actually grown in proportion to previous levels.

The educational level of the population in general, and in rural communities in particular, remains very low. Morazán sustains an illiteracy rate of thirty-four percent. Students in a sub-standard school system scrape by with a bare minimum curriculum designed to produce conformist *employee types* and then graduate into a society that has no employment opportunity.

The family, as a structure of society, has been greatly fractured by the war and currently by the continuing migration in search of economic opportunity. This situation reinforces the traditional *macho* dynamic that existed previously, with men having numerous extramarital relationships resulting in recognized as well as unrecognized offspring.

The macho element, however, must be put in the perspective of its counterpart, the matriarchal system commonplace throughout rural El Salvador. In Morazán, thirty-nine percent of head of households are women. Many times the matriarchal family unit is formed of siblings fathered from various, temporary relationships with the mother. It may contain two or more generations of unwed mothers. The tacit acceptance of this system results in a high rate of adolescent pregnancies and motherhood.

The growing social problems of the post-war generation reflect the stop-gap measures applied during the reconstruction effort. Social and economic programs were focused on the basic material needs of resettling communities, national infrastructure and public services. They did not begin to address root causes of poverty. The result has been a replication of the old cycles, but with an ever growing population and the added element of a steady flow of deportees with their vices and gang connections.

The other side of the coin, of course, is the tremendous potential and opportunity presented by the high percentage of young people in the Salvadoran society. They are a friendly people who are very quick to learn, willing to work hard and when given the opportunity, will excel in all fields of activity. The key, it seems, is access to opportunity.

Responsibility

I do believe the world is far too full
of far too many institutions
which we have created as a means of avoiding
responsibility.

"Someone should do something about that" and "Isn't
there some program around to handle that?"

We say,
as we turn away,
embarrassed to have come upon such an untidy
problem.

I may not have
the time, resources and power
to change the world,

Nor the wisdom

But

I Am

Responsible

For Everything

That Happens Around Me

"When I notice something that should be done, I've just been given the task of doing something about it."

I do not recall exactly where I read that, years ago, but it has always stuck with me. That philosophy, coupled with the Native American teaching of *leaving the land untouched or improved as you pass through,* strikes me as a much more efficient way to resolve our social and economic problems than to create centralized and specialized institutions.

Our penchant for relying on *experts* and public institutions is nothing more than the desire to sanitize our own little bubble of a world and turn our gaze away from our own responsibility. *Out of sight, out of mind.*

"My taxes pay for that," is an excuse without credibility even for the person using it. When have tax-funded public institutions ever solved more problems than they have created?

Inability is another inexcusable excuse. Anyone with firsthand knowledge of a problem possesses much more ability to resolve it than an Ivory Tower Expert flown in from the outside.

It comes down to a simple choice, jump in and get my feet wet and my hands dirty or retreat to my ever-shrinking bubble world, with the hope of not being noticed.

Amún Shéa

"The Poor will Always be with you!"
A Declaration of Sad Reality,
or a Challenge?

Poverty certainly has become
a Major Growth Industry,
Full of Experts, Studies, Flow Charts,
and Excuses

Vested interest in a growing cliental!
Corporate Projections and Slick Ad Campaigns
Promise More Bang for your Buck!
How Many Children can you feed
for the Price of a Starbuck's Coffee or a Night on the Town?

The Poor will Always be with Us.
More than Enough to go Around.
And with our Projections for the next Five Years
we'll have More.
Not Less!
So save ahead!

Time flies by! I've been around long enough to watch children that played in the dusty streets of the Colomoncagua refugee camps grow up. I now see their children playing in the dusty streets of the resettled communities of Morazán. I see the same imaginative play, the same happy faces, only now there are many more. The cycle of life repeats itself, once again. For years I have watched the series of large scale stop-gap reconstruction and development projects and programs come and go in Morazán, as well as the rest of the country. Unfortunately, without having much lasting effect.

My opinion is that the focus has been on symptoms rather than the root causes of the problems. A strong, long term emphasis in education was a major missing element in these programs. Perhaps too long term for many. Not immediately stimulating enough to get a bang-up fundraising campaign up and running. The fundraising world goes through fads, phases and currently popular catchwords, often resulting in local organizations chasing after the latest available earmarked fad project. Like trying to catch butterflies on a windy day.

A dilemma is caused by the dynamic of *beneficiary targets groups* as projects for outside experts, who accept no input or decision making from the local population. This of course is made possible by the low academic and cultural level of the local population. That fact presents them as objects for outside intervention and never subjects of their own transformation.

With this obvious void to fill, I began the process of getting back into the humanitarian or social side of life. My thought was to build a school, with the purpose of instilling the capacity and desire in young people, to forge their own destiny and to be a positive element in the building of community.

I mulled over the idea for several years. Although I have gone out on the limb many times, the thought of stepping out into the unknown territory of this important need seemed too far out of the range of my abilities. Over the years I had talked about this idea with many friends and with visitors to the hotel who seemed inclined to support the people of Morazán. The motivation to move from thinking and talking to actively pursuing it came from the needs of my own children. That, of course, may be understood as having a goal to build a school for my children. However, it does go a bit further.

For over twenty years I had been with the people of El Salvador. Starting with the refugees in Honduras, to emergency work in San Salvador with the war displaced, through the transition period to the ending of the conflict and then as a businessman. I shared laughter and joy as well as tragedy and loss. I have had a few adventures on the way. But, it was always as an outsider. I was always free to pick up and leave at a moment's notice.

My children changed that. Now, I have a stake in the future of El Salvador. Any commitment I may have had before pales in comparison. I can try to protect my children from society or I can try to change society as my children grow up in the real world.

And so it began. It took all of ten minutes, with a local businessman, to get a donation of twenty-two acres of land for the school. With a group of friends and acquaintances, who had become interested in the proposal, we formed a public charity in the US. The Perkin Educational Opportunities Foundation was founded and we started a school.

Amún Shéa, meaning "land of seedlings" in the original Lenca Potón language spoken in Morazán, was chosen as an appropriate name for the educational center. We began the school activities in a building borrowed from the municipality and went through the hoops to obtain accreditation from the Salvadoran authorities.

Non-alignment is a crucial policy of the foundation and Amún Shéa, although it may actually prove to be an obstacle for fundraising. El Salvador has experienced quite a lot of division. Political alignment permeates practically every level of social interaction.

Many people ask if we are building a *Christian school.* While Christian principles, morals and ethics, as primary rules of social interaction are essential, if we define ourselves as such, we would have to define religious alignment and that would instantly shun half of the population in Morazán.

Religious affiliation was equated with political alignment during the conflict. Churches were unable to remain detached from the daily reality experienced in their communities. In urban centers, believers had options within their own denomination from which to choose a parish or church which best suited their convictions.

Those options did not exist in rural areas. Many of those uncomfortable with the stance of the Catholic Church with regard to social activism converted to one of the evangelical denominations which were proliferating at the time largely through support by US protestant organizations. This resulted, in general, with the Catholic Christians being aligned with the left, and the Protestant or Evangelical Christians firmly aligned with the right.

In our search to find a solution to this dilemma, we began a relationship with an indigenous organization. The thought was to employ the moral and ethical standards that predated Christian divisions. That failed on two fronts. It gave the impression of looking back rather than forward, *too much smoke and feathers*, and put our accreditation process with the

Educational Ministry in danger. The organization itself was allegedly much too organically aligned with the left.

The concept is that if we seek help from established non-governmental organizations in the area, we lean left, and if we seek support from the governmental bodies, we lean right. The new reality of the left winning the executive branch does not modify that dynamic; it only interchanges the right and left. Non-alignment does not attract a lot of support.

I myself am somewhat of an enigma to many people in the area. To those on the right, I am probably a leftist because of my background and to those on the left: I must be a capitalist, because of the hotel business.

To have an ex-mayor of the ARENA party, as part of the Foundation, is even more confusing to many, especially given the number of left leaning teachers we have at the school.

Even the development of teaching methods is subject to unnecessary labeling. We borrowed from methods used by Waldorf, Montessori and others, but modified those methods to meet the current needs in Morazán. The result is a school without a label, and purposely so.

Amún Shéa is a concentrated effort with a limited number of students. There is no inclination to take over the task of the Salvadoran Ministry of Education, but rather to build a strong working model of an improved educational system which may be copied or incorporated into the national system. Indeed, on paper the curriculum of the Educational Ministry is academically sound, although it does lack right brain hemisphere exercise and reduces history to civics. The problem is in the implementation of what is on paper, with an overstretched budget, a deficit of infrastructure and teachers that are the product of an emergency *quantity over quality* educational system.

Our goal is to assist in the formation of a group of people capable of creating their own opportunities, making their own decisions and taking responsibility for themselves and their communities. Perhaps we'll create our own label along the way.

On Behalf of the Community

With the best intentions, individuals and groups will often use the phrase *on behalf of the community*. Often related to projects or development programs in war affected areas of El Salvador, the intent is to convey the community's desire for assistance or project their point of view.

I will admit that this self-appointed representation *on behalf of community*, causes a knee jerk, negative reaction in me. I have had the privilege of watching the civilian population of Perquín grow from 4, Torola from 6, San Fernando from 5, Arambala from 0 and El Mozote from 0, to the present day population centers they have become. I assisted in forming their organizations and obtained the project support for their initial subsistence and growth. Yet, I would never consider speaking on their behalf.

If nothing else was *won* during the war, people speaking up for themselves was a definite gain and they can do it very well, thank you. During the late 60s through the 80s, the need existed for some brave souls to stand up and *speak for those without a voice.* Most of them paid for that with their lives but they did make the difference. That's precisely why it is no longer needed. It is a throwback to the past. It is anti-evolutionary, anti-democratic and, in my opinion, anti-revolutionary. Communities are made up of individuals, not masses to be used for the sake of an argument or as cannon fodder, *good intentions* notwithstanding.

In El Salvador, traditional use of the term *community* more often than not is divisive, not inclusive, an attempt to separate the population into two camps: the *good and disenfranchised from the predators.*

Well-intentioned foreign organizations often choose a local organization to work through. Many of these local organizations are formed along political, religious, economical or clan lines and always have a deeper base than meets the eye. This phenomenon is one of the primary reasons a new type of organization is needed, one that is focused on community, not sectarian, enrichment.

The Brightest and the Best

That is a very innovative selection process up North to get the type of foreign workers needed.

First, set up the prize. Earn as much in one hour as for a whole day in El Salvador. Second, set up the obstacle course. Practically no visas, dangerous route through Guatemala and Mexico, jump the fence and a high-risk desert run at the end. Once there, faced with illegal status and immigration roundups as the order of the day.

Maybe there ought to be a new Statue of Liberty on the Rio Grande, dividing Texas from Mexico. It would have to be updated, of course, modeled after Britney Spears or the latest iconic *talent*, with her belly showing. The inscription reading "*give me your tired, your poor...*" would also need a little updating.

It should read *"Give me your most daring, your fittest, those willing to take chances. Give me your initiative, your future, your brightest and best."*

With around two million Salvadorans in the States, the largest national product is the remittances they send home. In sheer numbers, that workforce probably compares pretty much with the workforce left in El Salvador.

The Darwinist selection of those who go north, however, results in a quality unbalance within the two groups, at least at the gumption level.

It is probably too early to speculate on changes to the gene pool, but we are left working with those left behind.

The Gangs of El Salvador

The growing phenomenon of violent gangs in El Salvador and the US is one that requires a good hard look. On the surface, it is simply terrifying, and generally viewed as a law-enforcement problem to be dealt with by tough laws and tougher enforcement. Below the surface, however, there is a complex series of questions regarding the structure of society itself.

In many ways the *gang structure* is modeled after counterparts found within the social and economic structurcs of El Salvador, as well as many other parts of the world. Understanding the problem cannot be equated with excusing violent behavior, but until root causes within the social structure are uncovered and dealt with, the law-enforcement aspect will continue to multiply.

Closed circles of power exist at all levels of society. In El Salvador, even the new car market is controlled by one such group. Each member represents a particular make of vehicle and they allow no competition. You will not find competing Toyota, or any other, dealerships in the country. The same monopolistic practice occurs on all levels of business, from finance to commerce to utilities. Programs to alleviate poverty, such as donations of seeds and fertilizer, are carefully divided out according to political affiliation. The message is clear, either belong to a group or you will flounder on your own.

The concept of becoming a member of a group is instilled at a very young age. Your place in society often depends on the *tanda* or group of classmates you go through school with. A *tanda* sticks together for life, exchanging favors and influence for the benefit of the group members. At the professional class level in the cities, parents very carefully choose the most suitable school for their children. The decision is based more on which families are represented in that school than on academics.

I know an architect in San Salvador who belongs to a second level circle. It consists of the support personnel for a fairly small but wealthy power group. He is making tremendous economic sacrifices to keep his two children in the same foreign language school as the children of his superiors. His hope is that they will be able to make the jump to the next level.

The origin of gangs is no secret. The lack of political power in marginalized communities creates the need for a form of self-defense and identity for inhabitants who find themselves shunned by the larger society. This dynamic goes through ever widening cycles which maintain and reinforce the *us against them* mentality. This goes on until entire communities are considered lawless states within the state. The gangs become the de facto military government in these communities, excising *taxes* and dealing out *justice*. The official police force falls easily into the position of the *opposing gang* and resorts to warfare tactics which only escalate the conflict.

All *gangs* have their distinctive uniform. The tattered torn look of the university academic, the power suit and accessories of the Wall Street Elite and the skin-head fashion of US law enforcement are all group identity signs. The Salvadoran street gangs have theirs also. Their uniform is their tattoos, which create the desired visual effect along the lines of the high black boots of the National Guard or the black Jeep Cherokees of the death squads. The effective *shock and awe* tactic of beheading and dismembering, implemented by the gangs, was learned and copied from the death squads of the 70s and early 80s.

While turf wars between rival gangs are shockingly graphic as they take place in city streets, they would seem to reflect what goes on in the corporate world of hostile takeovers and bloody turf wars for everything from banana plantations to oil fields. Many of our models serve to reinforce and give tacit approval to the gang structure. We have created a *survival of the fittest* societal mentality which applauds forceful strength. Opportunity exists for those who take it.

A young person growing up in a marginalized community has little to no chance of staying out of a gang. Indeed the gang structure replaces the missing family unit and gives identity where none existed before. Many times the young person leaving rural areas in search of opportunity in the urban areas of El Salvador or the cities in the US, needs to make a practical decision. They must decide if they will join a gang or live a potentially very vulnerable, individual, existence. The rising xenophobia and marginalization faced by these young people, in many places, actually encourages them to seek the protection of a gang.

Opportunity and identity seem to be the key to attacking the problem of street gangs. We must look at inclusion rather than rejection of entire communities that *don't fit in.* Declaring open season on any kid with a tattoo is a declaration of war and if we continue down that path, we will soon have to accept them as a belligerent force and be forced to a negotiation table to hammer out a peace accord.

Why is it that we don't seem to learn from the past? Different uniform, different flags, different cause, same kids dying.

A truce between the Salvatrucha and M18 gangs, in March of 2012, reduced the homicide rate in El Salvador from fourteen to five per day. The truce was mediated by the Catholic Church and Raul Mijango, an ex-ERP field commander. Surprisingly, well perhaps not, a lot of controversy was generated by the truce. The government admitted negotiating better conditions in the jails for gang members in exchange for a reduction in the homicide rate. This caused an uproar among businessmen and the general population who continue paying extortion to the gangs. They saw the deal as filling a propaganda need by the government to show improvement to the outside world. The fact that the former homicide rate reflected gang members killing off gang members was seen as good riddance.

There are many interests involved; many more than meet the eye. The labeling of the Salvatrucha gang as a "transnational criminal organization" by the US Treasury Department, in October of 2012, adds a new dimension to the process.

There are obvious parallels in this situation with the failed attempt to end the war by President Duarte during the '80s. Too obvious to see, apparently.

Why stay in El Salvador?

What law exists for me?
I reject most norms, perhaps all norms.
Free of law!

Love thy neighbor as thyself
and
to thyself be true
the only keepers

But if I decide to remain in a society
built on a paradigm
crumbling as it is
with norms based on false beliefs and superstitions
AM I
compromised?

I am often asked why, or when, I decided to stay in El Salvador. Of course, many times the question is simply a conversation filler, with a simple rote reply expected, "I fell in love with a local girl and stayed."

I do not like rote answers, but if I launch into a full explanation of the subject, the questioner gets more than bargained for and further conversation ceases.

Actually, I never made a decision to stay. There has always been one more activity interesting enough to keep me around. Time has gotten away from me but I am only reminded of that fact when I look in a mirror or someone asks me my age. I have passed the tipping point of being in Central America longer than I lived in the States. That works out to about eighty percent of my adult life. Perhaps no decision was a decision, although I despise passive or default decision making.

While growing up I admired the pioneer spirit of the Wild West period and lamented the lack of new frontiers to explore. My brothers and I would go through the classified ads in outdoor magazines and plan to go to the Canadian Wilderness, Alaska or even the North Carolina swamps. There we would either stake out a claim or just buy cheap land. The challenge was to go somewhere that was completely undeveloped and build a life.

Life in the States seemed to tame, too planned, too restrictive and with much too much concern about insurance, job security, health care and retirement.

Where was the raw un-edited life to be found? Are we only here to maintain ourselves for as long as possible?

In the States, we hit our peak in the 60s. The assassination of Kennedy, related or not, marked the end of an era of progress and the beginning of a plateau of maintenance.

As a society, El Salvador is in an adolescent stage, with limitless love, unfettered tragedy, untamed energy and volatility. There is no way to go but up. The chance to participate in some small way in the growing-up phase is an attractive challenge. It's not the Wild West, of course, but it does provide the opportunity to build *something out of nothing.*

Epilogue

Twenty years have passed since the signing of the Peace Accords, although it seems like yesterday. Those who made it through the war have moved on with their lives. Some have disappeared into the background. Others have rebuilt a *normal* life. More than a few continue to work toward creating change and progress, albeit with less lethal methods.

It is impossible to stay in touch with everyone and there is no real reason to do so. Now and then I run into someone who looks vaguely familiar and if they look back with that same searching gaze, we'll talk and remember and somehow become younger in spirit. Very often a detail will come out, making sense of an incident long past. Human nature, once restricted by discipline and loyalty to the greater cause, surfaces and fills in the gaps left in history.

Some of us get together on occasion. Inevitably, the talk turns to the war. If a helicopter happens by during the conversation, the instinctive reaction by at least one of the present leaves the rest of us in laughter. Sheepishly rising from the floor, the comment is, "I thought I was over that."

All of us were marked in some way. Some with obvious missing limbs or battle scars. Some still carry bits of shrapnel. Others bear the more difficult invisible scars.

I carry one of those. I am well aware of at least one. I haven't dug below the surface yet to see exactly what it is. A few of the folks I worked with died during the war. That's normal because that's what war is about.

But in 89, practically everyone I knew from the cooperatives and communities went down to San Miguel. They went as militia during the offensive and got themselves killed. *I can't remember a single name.*

Even though I worked with them for several years, the names were gone as soon as they died. I never placed much importance on it, thinking it was a quirk of some kind. Ok, some type of denial. I should take a look at it one of these days because it might be an important piece of who I am. It may help explain why I tend to ignore people and things that are not part of what I am focused on. Or maybe that's just me.

The Hotel Perkin Lenca is doing well. It was put at considerable risk by diverting cash flow and taking out loans to get the school, Amún Shéa, up and running. In spite of the sluggish economy, the business is working its way out of that hole and has enjoyed steady growth.

Also, the modernization of the state in El Salvador has manifested itself in a proliferation of bureaucratic regulations and controls. We seem to have a weekly visit from one government agent or another. They are sent out to make sure we are paying enough taxes, not beating the workers and not serving out-of-date food. It is bothersome, but does have a positive side. We are well known and have become an icon of sorts. This once *crazy romantic project* has established itself firmly in the real world of El Salvador.

Amún Shéa is now in its fifth year as an innovative educational institution. The learning curve has gradually flattened out as experience is gained. The administrative structure is consolidating itself and is taking on more responsibility and is now independent of direct management by the Foundation. The student body continues to grow as we expand year by year. The novelty and misunderstandings of the new learning process have worn off. This allows more meaningful discussion within the educational community regarding curriculum and methods. Although the school still faces serious operational deficits and has many needs for capital investment, it has become a solid institution, ready to meet the challenge of creating a lasting change in one of the poorest regions in Central America.

The real world is not a pretty sight.
The colors mix and muddle. Concepts black and white turn to grey.
and fade away

Ideals untried by fire...such sweet innocence
So easy to take...and break

Ideas great and perfect in their conception
So easily soiled out here
in the real world

Immovable? Unchangeable?

Ode to Sisyphus pushing that rock uphill time after time after time

in the real world

Ideals tempered, Ideas tattered

bringing color back
into the real world

A safe sheltered upbringing, with its values and ideals, is a real blessing. Those of us who have had that privilege should be grateful, very grateful. It does, however come with a huge responsibility. Ideals are to be tested. Ideas are to be applied.

Out there, where failure is an option. Where fire is awaiting to temper and where perfect ideas are torn to shreds. Out there, where you can change reality.

Pop the bubble and hang on for the ride. It's worth it and it's why you came here.

Twenty-nine years ago, arriving as a young volunteer eager to help, the *we* and *they* were clearly defined. Right and wrong was marked out with unambiguous straight lines. Limits were firmly established.

The *we and they* is fairly muddled now. I often stop in the middle of a conversation to figure out which best applies. Interestingly enough, right and wrong are still clearly separated. However, they are no longer defined only by my head, but more so by my heart. Limits have become self-imposed excuses, a type of comfort zone and safety net. Of course they still exist, but get pushed back when they get in the way.

It's funny but that phrase "be in the world, but not of the world" ingrained in my upbringing has come back as a real truth. I no longer belong anywhere. It is impossible to *go back* to a world that only exists in my memory and impossible to get past being an outsider here. The concept has taken on new meaning. It can no longer be an excuse to hide away in the shelter while the rest of the world destroys itself. It is more of a command: Get out there and do something, just don't sink so far into it that it takes your soul. Which gives weight to my father's adage, "remember now where you're from".

Out in the real world, you will discover that you do not have the corner on ideals and values. Many are putting life and limb on the line for what they believe. There are no safety nets, no safe havens for retreat. It's a humbling experience. It's an opportunity. It's life.

About the author

Ron Brenneman, a native of Delaware, USA, has been working with Salvadorans since 1983, in a combination of humanitarian assistance and private business. He currently resides with his family in Perquín, Morazán, in the mountainous northeast of El Salvador.

This is his first book.

The proceeds of PERQUÍN MUSINGS are donated to the Perkin Educational Opportunities Foundation, for the Amún Shéa School program. Please see www.peofoundation.org for more information.

Printed in El Salvador

First Edition

3,000